Cultivating Writers

Elevate your writing instruction beyond the skills to ignite the will

ANNE ELLIOTT

MARY LYNCH

Pembroke Publishers Limited

Dedications:

To John Parr Weston, my dear friend Cindy's father who sadly passed away this year. His mischievous grin, infectious laughter, and passion for all things fun are lessons of a life well-lived. And to my nieces Emma and Charlotte, may you be inspired to pick up the pen and record your own life stories. — A.E.

To my wonderful, inspiring mother—my first, longest and most valuable teacher of everything! Thank you for your dedication to critiquing, proofreading, and editing my writing for so many years. And to Mark and Jennifer who have become authors themselves in their respective fields. You make your writing mother proud! — M.L.

© 2020 Pembroke Publishers
538 Hood Road
Markham, Ontario, Canada L3R 3K9
www.pembrokepublishers.com

All rights reserved.
No part of this publication may be reproduced in any form or by any means electronic or mechanical, including photocopy, scanning, recording, or any information, storage or retrieval system, without permission in writing from the publisher. Excerpts from this publication may be reproduced under licence from Access Copyright, or with the express written permission of Pembroke Publishers Limited, or as permitted by law.

Every effort has been made to contact copyright holders for permission to reproduce borrowed material. The publishers apologize for any such omissions and will be pleased to rectify them in subsequent reprints of the book.

Library and Archives Canada Cataloguing in Publication

Title: Cultivating writers : elevate your writing instruction beyond the skills to ignite the will / Anne Elliott, Mary Lynch.

Names: Elliott, Anne M. (Anne Marie), author. | Lynch, Mary, author.

Identifiers: Canadiana (print) 20200195654 | Canadiana (ebook) 20200195670 | ISBN 9781551383453 (softcover) | ISBN 9781551389462 (PDF)

Subjects: LCSH: Creative writing (Elementary education)

Classification: LCC LB1576 .E45 2020 | DDC 372.62/3—dc23

Editor: Kat Mototsune
Cover Design: John Zehethofer
Typesetting: Jay Tee Graphics Ltd.

Printed and bound in Canada
9 8 7 6 5 4 3 2 1

Contents

Introduction 6

Chapter 1: Decluttering Writing Instruction 9

Underlying Causes for the Lack of Writing Will *11*
   Too Many Expectations *11*
   Too Much Structure *12*
   Too Much Instruction *12*
   Aiming Too High Too Soon *12*
A Call to Action *13*
Six Essential Steps *14*

Chapter 2: First Step: Develop Your Writing Life 15

Foster Your Own Writing Life *15*
   Writing Territories *17*
   Precious Time *17*
   Make Lists *18*
   Guests of Honor *18*
   Everyday Anecdotes *19*
   Express Yourself *19*
   Natural Wonders *20*
Share Your Writing Life in the Classroom *20*
   My Summer Pencil Path *20*
   Precious Pages *22*
   Author's Board *23*
Be a Writing Mentor *25*
   The Teacher Is Writing… *25*
   Teacher-as-a-Writer Show and Tell *26*

Chapter 3: Second Step: Tap Into Your Students' Lives 29

Writing Triage *30*
   Interest Inventory *31*
   Writing Survey *32*
   I Am a Writer Who… *32*
The Writer's Notebook *34*
   Notebook Tour *34*
   Cover Creation *36*
Mining Our Lives for Writing Ideas *37*
   Unforgettable People and Pets *39*
   Destination Known/Unknown *40*

Mining a Memento *41*
　　I Am From *42*
　　When I Was Young *43*
　　If You're Not From… *44*

Chapter 4: Third Step: Model the Habits of a Writer *52*

Wilful Habits *52*
　Celebrating Commitment *53*
The Habit of Finding *54*
　Tapping into Our Notebooks *54*
　Burning Questions/Cool Ideas *55*
　Reading to Spark Writing *56*
The Habit of Planning *What* *56*
　Format Flea Market *56*
　Format Tracker *57*
　Block Party *58*
The Habit of Planning *When* *60*
　Let's Make a Deal *61*
The Habit of Planning *Where* *63*
　All the Places We Love to Write *64*
The Habit of Acting: Thinking *64*
　Writing Is… *65*
　Writing Out Loud *65*
　The Writing Brain *67*
The Habit of Acting: Reading *68*
　Read-Alouds to Illuminate the Power of Writing *68*
　Replicating our Favorite Writers *72*
The Habit of Acting: Talking *73*
　Oral Storytelling *73*
The Habit of Acting: Sharing *74*
　Formal Sharing Techniques *76*
　Informal Sharing Techniques *77*
The Habit of Goal-Setting *78*
　Passionate/Proficient Writer Anchor Chart *79*
　Setting a Writing Goal *80*

Chapter 5: Fourth Step: Make the *Why* of Writing Visible *86*

Why Write? *86*
　Giving the Gift of Writing *87*
Writing to Express Thoughts and Feelings *88*
　Bursting Onto the Page *89*
　Inside-Out Writing *89*
Writing to Record and Document Memories *91*
　Memories Written to Music *91*
　Write that Down *92*
Writing for Pleasure and Enjoyment *92*
　Texts that Tickle *93*
　The Enjoyment Factor *93*
Writing to Clarify Thinking and to Share Knowledge and Experiences *94*
　Triple-C Card *95*
　Resident Experts *95*
　Writing-in-the-Real-World Interview *96*

    List the Learning *96*
    Using My Voice *97*
Writing to Become a Better Writer *98*
    Quick Writes *99*
    Prompt Power *99*
    Free Writing *100*
Writing to Become More Appreciative Readers *100*
Writing to Share Valuable Life Lessons *101*
Writing to Describe, Explain, Entertain, and Persuade *102*

Chapter 6: Fifth Step: Provide What Students Need to Write *104*

Writing by the Numbers *104*
    Gathering the Whole Class *104*
    Small Groups Unite *106*
    A Nook for One *106*
Tools of the Trade *106*
    Stowing Students' Stashes *108*
The Classroom Library *108*
    Appraising Your Classroom Library *111*
Documenting the Writing Journey with Writing Records *113*
    The Four P's: Publication, Permission, Presentation, Plagiarism *114*

Chapter 7: Sixth Step: Nourish the Will to Write *117*

Develop Your Writing Life *117*
    Work in Progress *118*
    Reading Our Writing Out Loud *119*
    New Releases *120*
Tap Into Your Students' Lives *121*
    Writing Status *121*
    The Writer I Was/The Writer I Am *122*
    Supplementary Seed Ideas *122*
Model the Habits of a Writer *123*
    The Habit of Finding *123*
    The Habit of Planning *125*
    The Habit of Acting: Thinking *127*
    The Habit of Acting: Sharing *129*
    The Habit of Goal-Setting *129*
Make the *Why* of Writing Visible *131*
    Connecting Our Writing to *Why* *131*
    Writing Rants *132*
    Author Reveal *132*
Provide What Students Need to Write *133*
    Staying Current *133*
    Writer Bio *134*
    Conference Call *134*
    Publishing Centre *135*
Maintaining Momentum *135*

Final Thoughts *139*
Professional Resources *142*
Index *144*

Introduction

Once upon a time, children roamed their neighborhoods, played on quiet streets, and ran through fenceless backyards with their gangs. Kick the Can, Hide and Seek, Red Light/Green Light, Mother May I?, Red Rover, and What Time Is It, Mr. Wolf? were just some of the games generated, organized, managed, and orchestrated by kids. Play occurred spontaneously, rules were negotiated, problems were addressed on the spot, and games ended when Mom hollered out the door or streetlights came on. But times started to change and, before we knew it, play was forever changed. The toy market exploded and became more financially accessible to families. Children's TV programs erupted beyond Saturday mornings. And organized sport, clubs, and lessons became mainstream. The authentic, organic, choice-driven play of yesteryear seemed to disappear. Now here we are in 2020, and staff rooms are filled with teacher laments about children unable to play without adult direction, guidance, and supervision. Kids now seem to be unable to

- generate ideas
- create something from nothing
- access the materials around them as resources
- use what they know to develop and organize themselves
- carry out a plan

To play, they must have the proper equipment, clear rules, someone keeping score, a referee, and a reward or trophy for the winner. Please don't get us wrong—children learn valuable life lessons and skills from organized sports and activities. We wonder if, in our quest to keep children safe, engaged, stimulated, and active, the pendulum has shifted so far that there is no longer time and space for authentic, organic, child-driven play. Incidentally, research now indicates the need for unstructured play that enables children to create, explore, and navigate their world independently:

> "Play nourishes every aspect of children's development… Play develops the foundation of intellectual, social, physical, and emotional skills necessary for success in

school and life. It "paves the way for learning." (The Canadian Council on Learning, 2016, pg. 2)

What we need is to strike a balance between the two scenarios: structured and supervised versus organic and free.

This evolution of play has connections to writing instruction. In the 1990s, Donald Graves, Don Murray, Lucy Calkins, Regie Routman, and others revolutionized our understanding of how students can see themselves as writers and are compelled to write prolifically. Their student-centred approach to writing instruction placed students in the driver's seat of idea generation, determining the format they would write, who their audience would be, and what pieces would be taken to publication. Students discovered

> I have something to say, my voice has value, and the decisions on how I say it are mine. My teacher is a support who guides me as a reader of my writing. They help me identify my voice and purpose; draw attention to areas of strength, places to clarify and improve; offer timely and specific feedback to consider as I develop as a writer.

Writing was authentic, organic, and choice-driven. Teachers taught the writer, not the writing.

But the winds of change started to blow within school boards and across the country. In all curriculum areas, the focus became standards, outcomes, and expectations that could be measured. The mighty gusts led to the emergence of a results-based system driven by testing scores. Our attention was thrust onto the expectations and skill-driven instruction and pulled away from student-driven writing environments. In the literacy world, the focus became creating a skilful writer who understood

- form (descriptive, narrative, persuasive, expository, etc.)
- format (story, poem, letter, report, etc.)
- writing traits (ideas, organization, sentence fluency, word choice, conventions, presentation)
- process (brainstorming, drafting, revising, editing, publishing)
- craft techniques

However, in our quest to do better for our students and to meet testing expectations, we suddenly became overzealous about teaching writing skills. We taught the writing, not the writer. The teacher had the lead in this production and the student took on a minor role. The teacher had agency and ownership over writing decisions; the student was expected to merely follow the script. As a result, a new kind of writer seemed to emerge in our classrooms—the skilful writer who was compliant and capable as long as they were given very specific instructions, guidelines, and parameters.

In conversation with colleagues, we discovered that we were not the only ones who were beginning to notice the shift taking place among our writers. Students were becoming more skilful in crafting text, but appeared to lack the desire to write freely or derive joy from this worthwhile endeavor. As teachers, we began to reflect on our own practice and reminisce about the days when we were more focused on developing a writer's sense of self, voice, ability to see ideas everywhere, and, above all, compulsion to write it down! We realized that we let go of critical practices that gave life to authentic writing and adopted a more formulaic approach that stifled students' abilities and drive to be independent writers. In our quest to create proficient, skilful, success-criteria–driven writers, had we left no time and space for authentic, organic, personalized writing? The self-driven writer seemed to disappear. It became apparent that we needed to address and invest in developing the will to write, along with skills. After all, what good are the skills if you do not have the will?

We longed for our students to see writing as a rewarding experience, to appreciate its potential as a pastime, to carry an enthusiasm for writing beyond the classroom. We knew these were worthwhile aspirations to have. What teacher doesn't dream for this to happen for their students? However, we were acutely aware that there were obstacles we would have to contend with in our quest to turn students on to writing. For example we wondered if our expectations and the text models we provided were too high, too soon. Did this contribute to our students feeling dissatisfaction and disappointment with their drafts? Some students enter our classrooms with a negative attitude about writing and their own ability, due to an overemphasis on writing conventions (e.g., spelling, grammar, punctuation, legibility). Others suffer from the misconception that, because writing takes effort on their part and requires revision, they are not capable. It's as if students expect their first draft to be their only draft, and having to revisit a piece of writing is evidence that they are not proficient writers. On the other hand, some students see little value in writing pursuits in their jam-packed schedules; some are glued to their phones and consider it an appendage.

But we were willing to tackle, tear down, or even catapult away these obstacles in our mission to create wilful writers. Transferring and turning writing ambitions into reality meant our explicit instruction had to directly address these goals. Skill-based writing instruction was simply not enough to ignite a writing passion within students.

In this book we offer classroom-based solutions that have been developed, tested, and refined over a number of years in classrooms. It is built around six essential steps:
1. Develop Your Writing Life
2. Tap into Your Students' Lives
3. Model the Habits of a Writer
4. Make the *Why* of Writing Visible
5. Provide What Students Need to Write
6. Nourish the Will to Write

Using these practices, you, too, can take writing instruction beyond an emphasis on teaching the skills to address the will. By amalgamating sound pedagogy from the past and present you will equip yourself to create a writing environment that merges these two critical components.

We have the responsibility, the obligation, and the duty to create an environment in which kids flourish into writers who have the skill *and* the will. In *Cultivating Writers* you will discover how to foster writing engagement through an active writing community. You will reflect on the way in which you currently teach the will of writing, and be inspired and motivated to incorporate new ideas and strategies into your practice—to do what you do even better, just as we have!

1

Decluttering Writing Instruction

Do you remember a TV program from the early 2000s called *Clean Sweep*? It focused on decluttering your home, and showed home owners sorting their items into three distinct piles: Keep, Sell, and Toss. And now there are many similar shows: *Clean House*, *Mission Organization*, *Master the Mess*, and the Netflix sensation *Tidying Up with Marie Kondo*. If you're like us, you are amazed and sometimes appalled by the amount of stuff people accumulate and allow to dominate their spaces. However, by the show's end, we are looking around our own homes with a critical eye to cleaning up and clearing out.

What should we keep and what can we toss? These are challenging decisions that require a measuring stick. For Marie Kondo, the question when deciding what to keep is always "Does this spark joy?"

> *Mary*
>
> When I had to determine what items I would keep following my father Dan's passing, the task was exceptionally challenging. The decisions were wrought with emotion, memory, and connection. Not all items could be kept, nor were important to keep. The essential question when making the choice was "What kindles a treasured memory of me and my father?" With this question at the forefront, selecting treasured items came to mind instantaneously. My father's Tilley hat, which he never went anywhere without, always perched on his head during his regular visits on my front porch, was definitely a keeper. It now sits prominently and proudly in my kitchen for all to see as a daily reminder. From his treasured Santa Claus collection, I selected an old-fashioned rendering of the jolly old fellow that reminded me of Christmases past. Lastly, my children requested the carved wooden checkerboard on which games were played with their Papa. Treasured keepsakes all.

As teachers we are routinely faced with the question of what to keep and what to let go. We accumulate a lot of "stuff": the curriculum, school-board expectations, initiatives, programs, lesson frameworks, instructional strategies, resources—the list is endless. And like that of a homeowner, our spaces and minds can become cluttered and muddled. We need to give ourselves permission to stop, reflect, evaluate, modify, and let go, with our decisions based on sound research and pedagogy and our classroom practice. By merging these two fields of understanding, we can make informed decisions in the best interest of our students on what we should keep and what we can let go.

These are the exact questions we asked ourselves when reflecting on our writing programs. The work of Gail Tompkins and Lori Jamison Rog highlighted the stages of the writing process and the various writing forms/formats, while Ruth Culham brought the writing traits to life and offered mini-lessons to teach them explicitly. Ralph Fletcher, Lynn Dorfman and Ann Cappelli, along with Elizabeth Hale, illuminated the importance of lessons focussing on craft techniques. We used their tangible lessons and activities with our students and ensured we provided ample opportunities for practice. Our writing conferences provided the evidence that our students were becoming skilful writers due to our explicit instruction.

> This ground-breaking research changed our understanding not only as writing teachers but also as writers ourselves. Our pedagogy and practice was raised to a new standard and our students grew and developed as strategic writers. The innovative work of these literacy leaders elevated our beliefs and practice. We are grateful for their research and contributions to literacy instruction.

When we took the time to stop and critically examine our classroom practices through the lens of writing, our observations indicated that most students were able to

- follow the writing process to produce grade-level text
- identify the forms of writing (e.g., narrative, descriptive, expository, persuasive)
- include the specific features of various formats in their writing
- craft pieces that utilized the traits of writing
- employ a variety of craft techniques

We were pleased to see students who were capable, skilful writers. Our writing instruction had met its mark. Bull's eye!

However, to be transparent, we were disheartened to also discover students who

- were not excited to write ("Ugh! Do we have to write today?")
- didn't talk proudly about the text they were writing ("It's not that good.")
- were not aware of their writing territories (i.e., ideas) ("I don't know what to write about.")
- found free writing overwhelming and challenging ("What do you want me to write? Aren't you going to tell me?")
- were not invested in revising their work ("It's fine just the way it is. I like my first draft.")
- were unaware of the rewards and value of writing in their life ("I only write at school and when given an assignment.")

It was clear that many of our capable, competent writers were the farthest thing from passionate writers, that their will to write was lacklustre or even nonexistent. They didn't seem excited about writing. They didn't derive joy from writing freely. They weren't actively on the lookout for their next writing idea. They were simply going through the motions to meet the assignment criteria. Think about your own classroom—does this sound familiar?

In our travels across Canada and the United States, attending and presenting at various conferences, we have heard teachers express similar concerns regarding writing will. In fact, Ontario's Education Quality and Accountability Office statistics show that writing rates in Grade 6 have remained relatively stable going back over several years (i.e., 2017–2018: 78%; 2016–2017: 80%; 2015–2016: 79%; 2013–2015: 80%). This data does indicate that the majority of our students can write at the provincial standard. However, as part of this standardized testing, students are also asked to complete a writing survey. In particular they are asked to respond to the following prompt: *I like to write*. Since 2012/2013, Grade 3 girls reporting that they like to write "most of the time" fluctuates between 54% and 60%, while the percentages for boys range from 40% to 45%. When looking at this criteria for Grade 6 students over the same time period, the girls reporting that they like to write most of the time varies between 51% and 55%, while the boys range from 28% to 31%. From these statistics it is clear that our students' self-reporting of liking writing decreases over the years from Grade 3 to Grade 6, and that the percentages of our students reporting liking writing "most of the time" consistently and alarmingly lags behind their ability to write. Even though provincial, board, and classroom data indicate that writing achievement is relatively reasonable, the same cannot be said for writing engagement. Standardized testing reveals skilful but not wilful writers.

These statistics become more concerning when you consider the far reaching benefits of writing. In the *Handbook of Writing Research*, MacArthur, Graham, and Fitzgerald summarize the power of writing as

> one of humankind's most powerful tools… Writing makes it possible to gather, preserve, and transmit information widely, with great detail and accuracy. As a result, writing is integrated into virtually all aspects of our society… [and] provides an important means for personal self-expression. (2006 p. 1)

"Writing is a significant literacy activity in modern life that enables individuals to accomplish a variety of personal, intellectual, occupational, and recreational goals. It has been demonstrated, across a variety of investigations, that writing activities yield a number of intellectual, physiological and emotional benefits to individuals."
— M. Smith, www.niu.edu

As educators, we understand the vast and varied benefits of writing. In particular we know that writing enhances our ability to think critically, to understand concepts more deeply, to facilitate the formulation of our own ideas, and to construct rational arguments. We recognize that writing calls on us to be problem-solvers, creative thinkers, and effective communicators. There's no denying it—cultivating a writing life has long-term benefits.

Underlying Causes for the Lack of Writing Will

Too Many Expectations

In our province, the Ministry of Education outlines overall and specific expectations for each subject area: Mathematics, Language, Science, Social Studies, Music, Drama, Dance, Visual Arts, Physical Education, and Health; Grades 4–8 have French as well. Because the curriculum is so immense, teachers strive to make every moment count and to ensure that their instruction is directly linked to curriculum. In Language alone, there are 75 specific expectations. Of the 25 that specifically target writing, none—zip, zero, zilch—address student interest and motivation to write, nor do any explore the benefits and value of writing. Every single one focuses on students acquiring the skills.

Too Much Structure

In our quest to effectively model and deconstruct specific text forms and formats, have we adopted a spoon-feeding approach to writing instruction? We wonder if we have taken on the role of ultimate decision-maker in our desire to efficiently determine if students have demonstrated mastery of skills.

Today you're going to write a descriptive letter about winter in Canada to a friend who has never experienced this season before. As the teacher I tell you the form you're writing (descriptive), the format (a letter), the topic (winter in Canada), and the audience (a friend). I will even provide you with a template to plan with (i.e., a web) and I will set the time frame within which you are expected to complete this assignment. I'll be sure to share with you the success criteria which I will use to assess your piece. Ready, set, write!

This example may seem extreme, but we've all been there. Certainly there is a time and place for on-demand writing, and structure has its benefits. But what happened to choice, play, and experimentation? These are the catalysts for young writers to discover their unique voice, to come to understand that their thoughts and ideas have meaning, and that their writing has purpose and power. So let them choose, let them select, let them decide. After all, it is their writing!

Too Much Instruction

A mini-lesson connected to a read-aloud and modeled writing doesn't sound like a tremendous amount of instructional time within a writing block; it sounds manageable. However, far too often our mouths run away from us, our minis become maxis, and modeled writing consumes the entire writing block. Before we know it, time is up and students have had little if any time to write. Doesn't that sound wrong? Think about it: your child would never go to a piano lesson without tickling the ivories; your daughter would never go to soccer practice and not make contact with a ball; your son wouldn't go to an acting workshop and not take the stage and run lines. Why would we have students attend a writing class and not have them pick up a pencil? We have to let students write regularly—for the joy it, to embrace the challenge, to discover that it is messy work, to know that sometimes their writing will pour off the pen while other days it will merely trickle, to uncover their writing territories, and, above all, to know that their voice matters in our world. So give them real opportunities and long stretches of time to write.

Aiming Too High Too Soon

You don't run a marathon without tackling a few 10Ks, you don't take on decorating a wedding cake before icing a few cupcakes, and you don't end up performing on Broadway without first taking the stage in a few local theatre productions. So why do we so often ask students to produce a complete piece of writing without adequate play and practice? Could it be that, when we feel the pressure to have marks in our assessment book, we transfer that pressure to our instruction? In many cases we move too quickly from modeling to drafting, and to having students submit a final piece. We have unintentionally taken away writers' opportunities for practice with different topics, experimentation with various techniques, and time to apply essential feedback. It seems that every time a student writes something, it is expected to be handed in and assessed, given a grade, level, or mark. Can you imagine if every time you read something a running record was taken and a comprehension assessment was assigned? What impact would that have on your enjoyment, desire, and will to read? We are cognizant of the need to provide our readers with time to simply immerse themselves in the pleasure of reading with no strings attached. When it comes to writing, we seem to be caught in a cycle of write/assess, write/assess without giving our students the time to apply, develop, and grow as writers. Our students must be allowed to compose far more than we can ever provide feedback on and assess. Only that way will they develop their stamina, skills, and will. Our standards for young writers are too high, too soon. So close the mark book for a time, step back, and allow your writers to step up and write!

A Call to Action

With these concerns in mind, we realized that, in our quest to create the skilful, proficient writers outlined in the curriculum expectations, we had neglected to nurture the will to write. When we looked back on our instruction, we could not find any evidence that we explicitly explored the will to write with our students. We had clearly taught the skills. There was irrefutable evidence of that. But without a positive attitude and the motivation to use those skills, what good are they? Our new-found knowledge, instructional ideas, and mini-lessons crowded out what we previously identified as essential elements of our writing classrooms. We threw out what we should have kept, and our writers suffered the consequences.

The realization that we had contributed to the disappearance of the creative, independent writer that Calkins and Graves spoke so passionately about nurturing was startling to us. Steven Layne wrote that being a complete reader involves both skill (phonetics, fluency, comprehension, semantics, syntax) and will (interest, attitude, motivation, engagement) (Layne, 2009), and so does being a complete writer. To be complete, we believe that writers must possess both skill (knowledge of forms/formats, writing traits, process, and craft techniques) and will (interest, attitude, motivation, engagement).

In *Joy Write* and *Writing Workshop*, Ralph Fletcher calls on us to create environments in which writers have wide latitude to develop a love of writing and to recognize the value and importance of writing in their life. This plea is echoed by many literacy leaders, including Katie Wood Ray, Georgia Heard, and Ruth Ayres, who inspire us to think deeply and critically about the importance of turning students on to writing. Surrounded by experts who have inspired us, we reflected on our practice. While we were pondering how to develop the will to write in our students, the following questions emerged:
- How do I develop a writing community among my students?
- How might I create a classroom environment in which students feel accepted and comfortable taking on the risks and challenges required to develop as a writer?
- How can I ignite a desire to write in a way that prepares students to enter the classroom with enthusiasm and purpose?
- How can I share my passion for writing with my students? If I do not identify as a writer, what impact will that have on developing my community?

- How will I share my writing life with the class in a way that will turn them on to writing? If I do not see myself as an active writer, how could I begin to cultivate a writing life?
- In what ways can my students embrace writing outside of school?

In our relentless pursuit for answers, we embarked on a quest to find solutions for our students, ourselves, and our colleagues. These solutions have become our core beliefs for developing and fostering the will to write in students. We believe students must

- See writing as fun and enjoyable
- Understand that everyone grows and changes over time as a writer
- Realize that becoming a better writer takes time, effort, and energy
- See themselves as valuable members of our writing community
- Realize that we write for different purposes and audiences
- Understand that there is a world of text out there to be used as mentors
- Know that they have a writing voice and that what they have to say matters
- Uncover the vast number of reasons we write
- Discover their own writing habits
- Know that their teacher is a committed, keen, active writer
- Know that one of the defining characteristics of our classroom is that we are all authors

Six Essential Steps

Cultivating Writers offers you our best thinking and practical suggestions to choose from as you foster the will to write in your students. We are not offering step-by-step lessons, but rather presenting opportunities for you to create your own personalized community for the students in your class. We believe it's critical that your own voice comes out loud and proud. What you will find here are activities that honor what we believe to be the essential steps in creating a community that cares about writing:

1. Developing Your Writing Life
2. Tapping into Your Students' Lives
3. Modeling the Habits of a Writer
4. Making the *Why* of Writing Visible
5. Providing What Students Need to Write
6. Nourishing the Will to Write

These steps form the basis of the chapters that follow, where you will discover how to intentionally develop the will to write. We share classroom-based solutions that have been developed, tested, and refined to significantly change the writing culture in classrooms. We offer you tangible ways to foster writing engagement through developing an active writing community. By targeting your instruction, you will begin to build a foundation for writers who are motivated to write and who will support each other on their writing journeys. For us, the rewards have been transformative, and there is no going back. Our hope is that you will be motivated to adopt the belief that influencing will is as important as teaching skills. We are excited to share our best thinking with you. Let's go!

> "Once we know who we are and what we're about in the classroom, we become intentional in our teaching; we do what we do on purpose, with good reason. Intentional teachers are thoughtful, reflective people who are conscious of the decisions they make and the actions they take; they live and teach by the principles and practices they value and believe in."
> — Miller (2007, p. 4)

2

First Step: Develop Your Writing Life

Over the last two years we have invested in developing our yoga practice. Each week we visit our respective studios and are led through various asanas by our teachers. These yogis are exceptional instructors; they deconstruct each asana, and position students into optimal poses for development. They are committed to their own personal practice, dedicating time and energy to it. By attending the classes of their mentors and participating in conferences, they demonstrate an ongoing devotion to their practice. Our yoga teachers do not merely sit on their mat and call out instructions. They model, coach, affirm, and provide feedback. But more than that, they actually do yoga themselves!

So what does our yoga instruction have to do with writing? Everything! In *Writing: Teachers and Children at Work*, Donald Graves states

> We don't find many teachers of oil painting, piano, ceramics, or drama who are not practitioners in their fields. Their students see them in action in the studio. They can't teach without showing what they mean. There is a process to follow. There is a process to learn. That's the way it is with craft, whether it be teaching or writing, there is a road, a journey to travel, and there is someone to travel with us, someone who has already made the trip. (Graves, 1983)

You are the writing teacher in your classroom. You are directly responsible for creating the writing culture and climate. We believe your students deserve a writing teacher who is knowledgeable about the craft, process, and challenges of writing. Your students are entitled to a writing teacher who provides insightful feedback, tips, and suggestions. They are also worthy of a writing teacher who incites enthusiasm and passion for writing. We cannot say it any other way. You have to be a writer, even if it's in your own way!

Foster Your Own Writing Life

If you find yourself reading this and do not identify yourself as a writer, know that by acknowledging that fact you have taken the first step. And we would argue you are not alone. In casual conversations in schools with countless educators, we have been hard pressed to find teachers who identify themselves as writers. They are much more apt to proclaim themselves as passionate, dedicated readers. We wonder why. Can the answer be found in the structure of Western culture? Have we been lulled into consumption rather than production? Consider…when was the last time you sewed curtains? Knit a sweater? Made a dinner completely from scratch? It seems we have evolved into a society obsessed with convenience, immediacy, and ease. It is far too easy to be a consumer. Likewise, we would argue that we are socially more structured to be successful readers than writers. Our public libraries, book stores, and book clubs attest to this. We are happy to digest the toil and labour of other writers, and willingly enter their worlds to escape our own.

Let's be frank—writing is hard work. Writing requires us to face an empty page and live with our eyes wide open and our hearts unlocked. Not an easy feat, but ultimately worth the labor and investment. Dorothy Parker said, "I hate writing, I love having written." It takes time, effort, and energy to generate ideas, to craft sentences, to select words, to spell correctly, to write cohesively and coherently. Whew! Moreover, when we use our personal lives as fodder for our writing by putting our thoughts, ideas, and opinions on the page, we make ourselves vulnerable. However, it is only by doing the work that we become sensitive, empathetic and truly aware of the effort it takes.

We also believe that the word *writer* is weighty. It carries with it visions of Shakespeare, Ernest Hemingway, Margaret Atwood. We associate writing with Newberry and Caldecott awards, endorsements by Heather from Indigo and New York Times Bestsellers. When we think of ourselves in this company, we find ourselves lacking and inadequate, and are reluctant to attribute the label to ourselves. But in reality our students don't need Shakespeare, Hemingway, or Atwood. They need a writing model, someone who is willing to share their attempts, stumbles, and drafts as a fellow writer in the class. As Katie Wood Ray says, "You just have to write a little bit better than they do."

We believe that you cannot effectively teach the craft of writing if you are not a writer. By engaging in the work yourself, you know that it takes

- vulnerability to share your inner thoughts and feelings on paper
- confidence to believe your voice has value
- attention and mindfulness to be on the lookout for topics that interest and engage you
- perseverance to stay with the task till completion
- patience and trial-and-error to get the words onto the page in a way that is pleasing to you
- thought to make the endless decisions the blank page requires
- other writers' work to sometimes springboard your own
- mentors to elevate the quality of your writing
- commitment to develop the habits of a writer
- rereading, rethinking, and revising to polish a piece
- risk to share your writing with others

This understanding comes from experience. It sets you up to be the ultimate writing role model in your classroom. In *Write Beside Them*, Penny Kittle states

> I wasn't supposed to *be a writer*—just someone trying to write—like them. In fact, I was a better model because my hesitations and insecurities were just like theirs.

It was such a relief to know that I didn't have to be good at it; just trying it was enough… Doing the writing taught me what to teach. (Kittle, 2008, pg. 9)

Here are a few suggestions we hope will jump start and add fuel to your writing life. These ideas will support you in carving out time to draft text and provide inspiration for writing topics. Fostering a writing community means you yourself have to be a writer. Welcome to the club!

Writing Territories

Take a suggestion from Nancie Atwell's ground-breaking book *In the Middle* and examine your writing territories. Grab a pencil and piece of paper, or your phone, and for the next week track all the writing you do. Don't edit yourself: list everything from e-mails to grocery lists, text messages to letters, journal entries to notes to your family. Acknowledge and honor the fact that you actually write a fair amount and that you communicate a wide range of information for different purposes throughout a week. We think you'll be quite surprised to discover the sheer volume of functional writing you do on a daily basis. Come on, it's time to recognize the writer in you! No need to police the quantity and quality of your writing.

Precious Time

Each day we have a limited amount of time available to us to engage in tasks we need and want to do. The need-to-do list is extensive: work, making lunches, laundry, taxiing kids, helping with homework, cleaning, taking out the trash, cutting the grass, etc. And for teachers we would argue it is longer! Our need-to-do list expands to include endless hours of marking, lesson planning, book orders, field-trip forms, newsletters, phone calls to parents, etc. Inevitably the time required to complete these jobs eats away at the time we hoped to have for our want-to-dos: working out, chatting with friends, watching our favorite shows, baking cookies. Considering all these demands, it is incredible that our lunch is made, the dishwasher gets unloaded, laundry gets done, and lessons are planned. Our long lists do get done, or at least what matters gets checked off.

We believe that, as you embark on developing your writing life, you have to put writing on the need-to-do list. Begin by making a commitment to write 15 minutes a day (as Donald Murray instructs). Don't feel that if you haven't got an hour you can't invest in writing; you can start with mere minutes. After all, 15 minutes is half the time it takes to watch your favorite sitcom, shorter than a period of hockey, and much less time than it takes for your weekly grocery shop. To set yourself up for success, consider setting a specific time for writing each day. Maybe for you the best time is after a morning walk where you are immersed in nature, right before you fall asleep as you reflect on the day, or while waiting for your daughter to finish her hockey practice. If you purposefully plan your writing, it will get done, just like the dishes!

Make Lists

> *Anne*
>
> My Aunt Margie is a compulsive list-maker. The minute you identify something you need to pick up, purchase, or do, she whips out the little spiral notepad she keeps in her purse and starts drafting the to-do list. She is often heard exclaiming, "If it's not on the list, it doesn't exist!" and admonishing others when they forgot something, "You should have put it on the list."

Moorea Seal, the creator of the *52 Lists Project*, articulates,

> From scribbling down daily tasks, mapping out lifelong goals, or tallying up our top ten favorite songs, so many of our inner desires and thoughts are revealed through the lists we create. ... Lists can be tools for self-discovery, exploration, and plenty of fun too." (Seal, 2015, Preface)

We believe that lists serve many purposes, from functional to personal, and as a writing starter they are unintimidating, short, doable, and usually low-risk. So if the idea of drafting a poem or composing a mystery story makes your writing hand quiver, lists may be the perfect place to get your pen moving. For ideas, the internet billows with endless prompts, and entire books can be found in the journal section of your local book store.

Guests of Honor

If your family is like ours, you have a couple of colorful characters who are whispered about at family picnics and reunions, and lovingly reminisced about. Mary's Uncle Clark was one such fellow. Every letter he wrote was written in rhyme and signed off with a phrase linked to the content of the letter. Each conversation was filled with countless pieces of trivia, and all phone calls ended with "Cheerio–pip-pip and all that rot." Family members like dear Uncle Clark have unique mannerisms, quirks, and habits, and their life choices never cease to make us pause and ponder. We kindly describe them as "interesting" or "eclectic," and they are the perfect people to invite onto the pages of our writing.

We all have people in our lives who are a constant source of inspiration. We hold these individuals near and dear, and we sigh and smile whenever their name is uttered. Consider using a Guest of Honor as a stimulus for your own writing: place their name on the page and start jotting down your stream of memories and recollections. You'll be laughing and smiling before you know it and, who knows, their unique personality and anecdotes may serve as a springboard for later writing.

> *Anne*
>
> Betty Black is a dear friend of the family. Even at the ripe old age of 97, her sense of humor and fun prevail, her memories take us back to simpler times, and her attitude and outlook are utterly uplifting. She is steady as the sun, and her room at the retirement home is never empty, as people are naturally drawn to the mischievous gleam in her eye, her quick wit, and her kind words. I could write pages and pages about this remarkable woman.

Everyday Anecdotes

There was a time when taking photographs meant we had to cross our fingers and hope that the shot was clear, eyes were open, and the image was in focus. We then had to wait till all 36 photos had been taken before we could take the roll of film to the camera shop to get the photographs developed. Fast forward to today. Most cameras are now part of phones, enabling people to edit, crop, filter, and transform any image into perfection. And these images are plastered on Facebook, Instagram, Snapchat, and Twitter as sterilized and fashioned renderings of our lives. But while we are readily able to capture, save, and share our life moments, we wonder what we are missing in our desire to portray the perfect image. What have we omitted, cropped out, or deleted? We would agree with William J. Harris: "Neatness, madam, has nothing to do with the truth. The truth is quite messy, like a windblown room" (Digh, 2014). Yes, life is messy, but isn't it in the mess where the story really resides? So harness your inner Erma Bombeck, who masterfully wrote about the ordinary in a humorous way, and write about the true richness of your everyday life. The duck that took up residence in your swimming pool, the time you accidently drilled a hole in the kitchen table while crafting, the day you face-planted while walking home from work and the entire contents of your bag filled the street. Those are stories worth recording, remembering, and reliving. So embrace the mess of your life and capture these moments in writing. Be sure to include as many details as you can!

Express Yourself

You can't open a newspaper, turn on the TV, or browse Google without encountering op-ed pieces expressing opinions, thoughts, and ideas about issues affecting our world. These commentaries tackle difficult and often controversial issues, and serve as a cathartic release for the author. There is power in having your voice heard. The COVID-19 pandemic, political issues, climate change, poverty, and immigration are just some of the topics featured on the front page of our newspaper as we write. These broad issues may be ones that you, too, are compelled to speak up and out about. Or maybe your burning issues are closer to your heart and home: a family disagreement, bike lanes in your community, or the adjustment of becoming an empty-nester. Take a lesson from the journalist's work and think about what issues concern you, keep you up at night, and find their way into your conversations. Take a minute to express yourself and write about these issues. Experience the relief that occurs when you use writing as an outlet to have your voice heard, even if it's just by yourself.

Natural Wonders

Magnificent moments occur every day in our world, as Louis Armstrong sang in the timeless, classic song "What a Wonderful World." The Earth truly is a beautiful thing, a potent, infinite source of ideas. From crashing waves to a single drop of rain, from a majestic lion taking down a wildebeest to a robin tirelessly tugging a worm from the earth, the big and small captivate us equally. So stroll, run, or sit with all of your senses activated to fully experience the wonders of our world. Then grab a pencil and transfer these awe-inspiring moments onto the page.

> *Mary*
>
> I religiously carry my phone in a vintage fanny pack on my daily walks to have it handy to capture the glory of our world. These stolen images become ideas for me to write about long after the walk is over.

Share Your Writing Life in the Classroom

Charles Whitaker states that one of the best practices in developing writers is a teacher who writes. He argues that

> …by sharing their writing—particularly when it's in draft form—teachers model respect for themselves, for their students, and for the act of writing itself. They communicate that they are part of the writing community in the classroom and in the world at large and that they feel safe sharing this part of themselves. (Whitaker, 2006)

If we intentionally plan and devote time to this worthwhile endeavor, students will quickly discover that their teacher not only teaches writing, but is also a dedicated writer. They will see it when we write in front of them. They will hear it when we read our writing to them. And they will feel it from the energy we mindfully put into the room. It has to be said again: kids have to know and see that you are a writer!

In the pages that follow you will find activities that support you in actively sharing your writing life with your students. These lessons will

- ask you to go back in time and explore your past experiences with writing, the texts you wrote when you were young
- invite you to think about your own writing life as a child and as an adult
- support you as you reflect on the kind of writer you are (or are becoming)
- provide your students with the language and tools they will need to think about their own writing lives.

My Summer Pencil Path

Students will
- realize that their teacher cultivates a writing life outside of school
- see their teacher as a writer who writes a wide variety of texts for different purposes

At this point you may just be beginning to identify yourself as an writer. We usually save that title for people whose names grace the cover of novels, newspapers and bestseller lists. But take a moment to think about all the times you did in fact scribble something down on a slip of paper, jot a note, or tap away on the keyboard. You wrote *something* this past summer. Notes, letters, lists, texts, emails,

Depending on what text you choose to share, your students may discover that writing is sometimes small and personal, and sometimes has no other audience but the writer.

social media posts, journal entries, travelogues, poems, maybe even a short story. You wrote and therefore are a writer! One great way to help students discover that their teacher is a writer who writes a wide variety of texts for different purposes is by sharing with them what you wrote over the summer and why you chose to write it. A pencil path will tell your students all that and more.

1. Gather a variety of texts you have written to show the scope of writing you have done. Write the topic, format, audience of each text on a pencil template.
2. Use your writing sample and the Pencil Path template on page 27 to tell your summer writing anecdotes:

   As we begin this new school year we need to get to know each other better as a community of learners. I will be getting to know you and it's important for you to get to know me. One key thing I want you to know is that I am a writer. I've gathered some samples of the writing I did over the summer to share with you. Take a look at this small journal. It's actually a travelogue that I created to document my recent trip to Kenya. (Read short excerpt from your travelogue)

   So many incredible things happened within one day that I knew I had to take time before bed each night to record my memories or they would be lost forever. Do you notice that my entry shares what I saw, did, ate, and heard, the names of people I met and the feelings I felt throughout the day? When I read it now, that day magically comes back to life for me.

   This summer I also corresponded with my friend Jane who has moved to Beijing, China, to work at an elementary school. As she adjusts to a new culture and school we try to connect with each other a couple times a week. Our written conversations share tidbits of our lives while we are living on opposite sides of the world. Sometimes we share funny anecdotes of our day, ask each other for work-related advice, or even console each other when we are missing our face-to-face contact and unable to just grab a coffee and chat. (Share a few emails/texts)

3. As you share each anecdote, post the corresponding Pencil Path pencil cut-out to create a visual display.
4. We recommend that you share four or five pieces of your writing and then ask students to turn and talk about what they have learned about you as a writer. These ideas might be recorded on a chart.

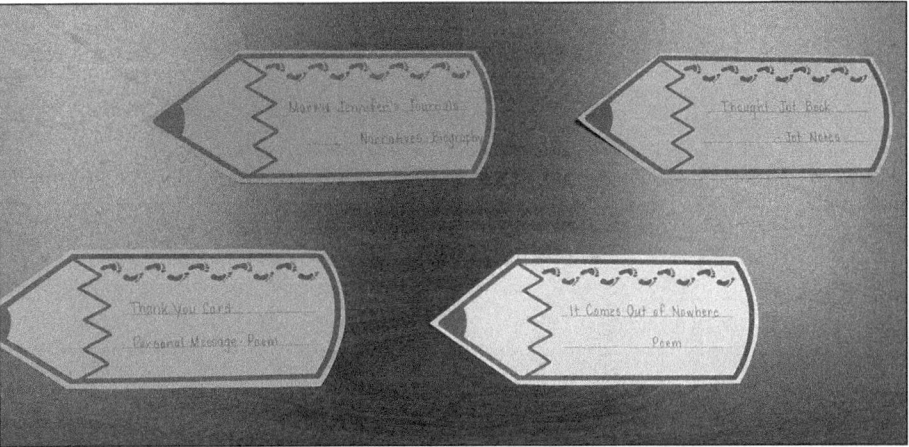

Share Your Writing Life in the Classroom

Student Link

During the first months of school, have students track their writing so that they too can create their own Pencil Paths. You might choose to gather pencil cut-outs from the entire class to create an eye-catching path of writing in the hallway. Not only does this celebrate your students' writing, but it also shares their writing accomplishments.

Precious Pages

Students will
- hear and see how writing affected their teacher when they were the students' age
- discover touchstone texts that stand out in their teacher's memory
- begin to create connections with writers outside of themselves (i.e., teacher, family, and friends)

Is there anything better than deciphering early student writing? It's a mystery to relish as you decode and solve. Mary treasures the early writing of her children Jennifer and Mark, and keeps these artifacts in scrapbooks as a fond memory of earlier days. The straightforward way young children express themselves, unconventional spelling, handwriting, and corresponding artwork bring a smile to her face. Children are often shocked when shown their early writing pieces. They are surprised to discover how far they have come and grown as a writer.

A powerful way for students to realize that you were once a young student just like they are now is to share a picture of yourself at their age. Talk about the texts you wrote in and out of school that stand out in your memory. Precious Pages will support students in discovering the writer you were at their age and help them form a personal connection with a younger you.

1. Dust off those old photo albums and look for a picture of yourself when you were around the same age as your students. Mount it on poster board and ensure there is ample display space around the image.
2. Consider what you wrote as a child in and out of school. Did you have a pen pal you corresponded with, a research project you were proud of, a treasured story composed by you for an assignment? Or were you an undercover writer at home, drafting humorous comics about a hockey prodigy, a travel journal of your annual summer road trip, or a top secret diary for your eyes only?
3. Look in those boxes of school memories and childhood mementos your parents forced on you when you moved out. Then hunt up a few of your writing keepsakes. If your writing was long ago sent to the burn pile or recycling plant, hit the internet and search for images that represent the writing you did. Gather/print a random selection (about four or five) that encompass the variety of texts you wrote.
4. Students will be intrigued from the minute they enter the classroom and see a photograph proudly on display. Watch their faces as the realization settles in that it is you in the photo. Once you and your students stop laughing at your childhood image, begin to share with them the story of your writing life at their age through the pieces you wrote. Display the texts around your photo one at a time and offer a brief explanation of why they are significant to you:

Do you have a place where you hide things you have written? A place where you store thinking that is for your eyes only? Is it on scraps of paper, in a journal, or in a diary with a lock and key?

Well, I remember one Christmas my Uncle Bill gave me my first diary. I clearly remember the excitement I felt over having a space and place to record my thoughts and feelings that was 100% PRIVATE. The tiny gold key fit perfectly into the lock and I squirreled it away in the back of my desk drawer where no one could find it. I fell in love with the nightly ritual of sitting on my bed and jotting down the highs and lows of each day. At the time, it allowed me to say things that

I wasn't brave enough or even allowed to say aloud. Now when I read it, I laugh at my ramblings and marvel at what I thought was important and interesting at the time!

A school writing project that stands out in my memory was when we had to create a product and craft a persuasive advertisement for it. I chose to market a fragrant hand soap in the scent of lilac to honor our family farm, which was called Lilacdale. I remember the attention I gave to word choice to appeal to the senses of the reader and the persuasive techniques I used to convince them they had to have the soap. I was proud of the final product and still am!

Student Links

- Have students think about the writer they are right now. Encourage them to share topics and formats that they gravitate toward writing and explain why.
- Another great link between home and school can be made by having students talk with their parents about their family's writing history. For example, does their family have special writing keepsakes from the past that they have held on to and treasure? Sharing these writing keepsakes will help foster your growing writing community.

Anne

I have letters that my great-grandfather and his brother wrote back and forth over many years, correspondences home during WWII, handwritten recipes, beautiful cards with personal messages, and even an ancestor's diary.

Author's Board

Students will
- see their teacher as an active writer who has written a variety of texts for different purposes over time
- discover that their teacher's writing life has evolved and changed over time with changing circumstances

Most days, students have the opportunity to witness their teacher write in their classrooms. More often than not, they are left thinking that we rarely if ever make a spelling mistake, that our writing is perpetually neat, that synonyms roll off our pen without the need of a thesaurus, and that idea generation is smooth and easy. They often see us seem to magically write lines of text with little difficulty, which is not surprising, considering we know ahead of time what we are going to write about and maybe even have written a first draft the night before. As a result, our students likely believe that we have always been strong writers with a natural ability to write, that we are able to generate ideas and spell words correctly with ease, that we have a solid command of different words and vocabulary, that we have always known what our writing preferences are, and that we write text effortlessly and share it willingly with others.

If we don't take students back in time and share with them our journey of becoming writers, they can be left with a lot of misconceptions. They need to be aware that every writer is on a journey, and that these excursions are sometimes filled with blue skies and paved roads, but at other times the skies open and the road is pitted with pot holes. So be transparent about your writing past:

- Did you struggle to generate ideas, to develop your thinking?
- Did you at times find writing a tedious task?
- Were there times you would ask to get a drink or take a bathroom break to avoid writing?

Or
- Do you have fond memories of making up stories and creating little books nightly?
- Did you have favorite authors and books you treasured that stimulated your writing?

For most of us, it is a balance of both; there are times when writing is truly enjoyable and other times when it is a chore, depending on the text, the time in our life, and the purpose for our writing. As teachers, mentor writers-in-residence, it is essential that we share our writing lives with our students.

1. Construct a storyboard timeline of your writing life in front of your students, sharing the purpose, format, and audience for your writing and the memories these text experiences evoke.
2. Consider tackling one section of your life each day to build a sense of anticipation and excitement. For example, different periods of your life you may wish to highlight: early writer, elementary student, secondary student, university/college student, parent, teacher, and adult. When constructing your Author's Board, it is the talk around your writing journey that is important. Talking points that might emerge from your timeline are:
- favorite pieces
- choice vs. assigned writing
- different topics and formats
- length of texts
- development of stamina
- purposes for writing
- sharing of text (audience)
- writing habits and preferred tools

Student Link

Have each student bring in a text that they feel good about having written. It might be a text from their early childhood or one they have written more recently, as long as they are proud of it and long to share with others. Or consider having students complete their own Author's Board.

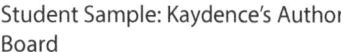

Student Sample: Kaydence's Author Board

Be a Writing Mentor

The Teacher Is Writing…

Students will
- realize that their teacher has an active, independent writing life outside of school
- see that their teacher is able to genuinely talk about writing because they write
- know that their teacher empathizes with the highs and lows of the writing process

At this point, you must be convinced that, as the mentor writer-in-residence, you must be a writer yourself. You must complete the same writing tasks you expect of your students and commit to responding to the same prompts and tasks in your own writer's notebook. It is now time to establish yourself as a fellow writer in the classroom community and be willing to share your own writing.

- Share excerpts of your personal writer's notebook with the class. Consider scanning specific pieces onto a large piece of paper with blank space around to welcome feedback from your students on your writing. This establishes you as part of the writing community and communicates to students that you cultivate a writing life outside of school.

A public display of your own writing creates a sense of energy and buzz around a potential text for students to read, provides students with a mentor and motivator, creates opportunities for conversations and dialogue, and holds you accountable to the class as a writer. When you do this, you distinguish yourself as a credible writer doing exactly what you are expecting your students to do. You can't fake this!

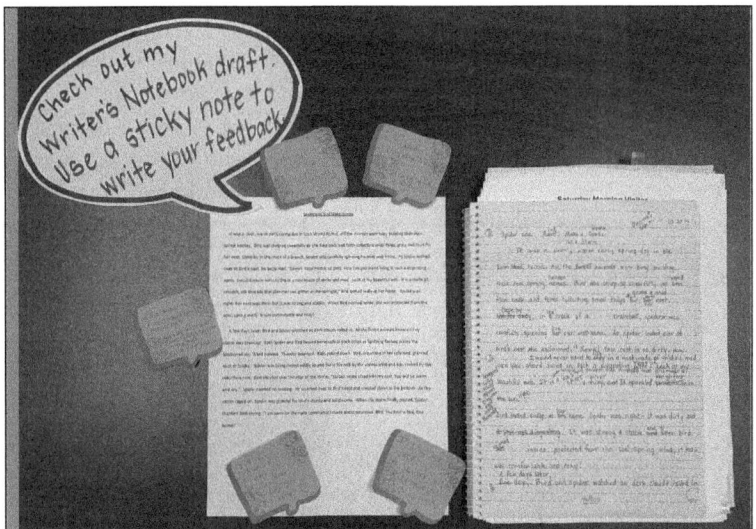

- When you put forward a prompt, post a picture, or share a powerful excerpt from a piece of text to stimulate student writing, be sure to grab your notebook, pick up your pen, and write too! This places you in the same position as the developing writers in your classroom.
- Playing with, exploring, and investigating specific craft techniques is an integral part of membership in a writing community. Alliteration, onomatopoeia, magic of three, repetition, brand names, and vivid verbs are just some of the craft techniques we want students to develop in their writing. We often do this in isolation, not as part of creating a formal writing piece. So when it is time to play with these techniques, be sure to be part of the game! This is another opportunity for you to show your writers that you, too, are developing your skills as a crafty author.
- Consider posting your most recent piece of classroom writing prominently in the room. For example, if students are involved in drafting fables, you, too, should be writing a fable and sharing your first draft publicly with your community.

Teacher-as-a-Writer Show and Tell

Students will
- identify and reflect on what they have learned about their teacher as a writer from previous lessons
- summarize the key attributes of their teacher as a writer

You might not realize it, but by engaging in the activities we have outlined, you have participated in writing show and tell. Your students have had the privilege of investigating a writing artifact—you! In making your writing life public, you have shown and told your students who you are as a writer in purposeful and intentional ways. Students have been shown and told the following:
- that *you* cultivate a writing life in and outside of school
- that *you* write a wide variety of texts for different purposes
- that *you* belong to a writing community; i.e., the classroom
- how *you* were developing as a writer at their age
- that *your* writing life has evolved and changed over time
- that *you* are a committed writer
- that *you* can genuinely talk about writing because *you* write
- that *you* value the mentor authors in the classroom library

This activity will be successful and powerful only if you have engaged in some or all of the preceding activities.

You have shown and told your students about you; now it's time to let students tell you what they have learned. It is time to pick the fruit of your labors, to uncover what your students have discovered.

1. Copy Give One, Get One Lists; see page 28 for templates. Distribute so that each student has one.
2. Encourage students to jot down at least three things they have learned about you as a writer. Here are some examples:

    She intentionally chooses words and often uses a thesaurus.

    She gets ideas for her own writing from other books.

    She has a Thought Jot book where she stores ideas.

    She writes about what she knows and cares about.

    She carves out time to write regularly.

    Her favorite genre to write is poetry, but most of her daily writing is functional.

    She has multiple pieces on the go.

    She enjoys sharing her writing with others.

    She prefers to write in pencil rather than in pen.

    She likes to write alone in her home office.

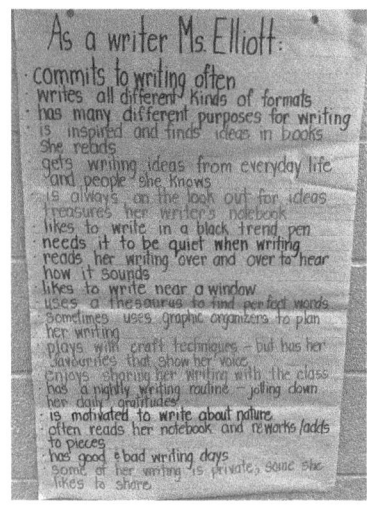

3. Once students have had a few minutes to think and have jotted down their ideas, ask them to travel around the room to give and receive ideas. Each student gives one fact about their teacher as a writer and gets one idea from a peer.
4. Use the information gleaned from students to create a chart listing the characteristics of you, their teacher, as a writer. Post this completed chart in the classroom to show that you value their thinking and learning, and that you make your beliefs as a writer and your writing life public. Most importantly, you can see what your students have discovered from previous lessons and your intentional sharing. This chart can grow and evolve throughout the year as students discover even more about their writing teacher.

Without a doubt our job is to inspire our students to become proficient, passionate writers. If we are to do that, we must share our writing lives with our students at the outset of the school year. There must be no question that their teacher is a writer and that each of them will become one too!

Pencil Path

Give One, Get One Lists

_____ as a Writer . . .

1. _____

2. _____

3. _____

4. _____

5. _____

6. _____

7. _____

8. _____

9. _____

10. _____

Name: _____

_____ as a Writer . . .

1. _____

2. _____

3. _____

4. _____

5. _____

6. _____

7. _____

8. _____

9. _____

10. _____

Name: _____

3

Second Step: Tap into Your Students' Lives

Long before the bell rings on the first day of school, teachers, administrators, secretaries, and custodians have been in buildings getting things in tip-top shape for the new school year. We know that teachers never seem to fully unplug from their chosen calling. During the summer, we can be caught reading the latest YA novel by Jason Reynolds, attending an area Nerd Camp conference, and hitting up every Dollar Store for classroom supplies over the summer months. We have also spent countless hours daydreaming about classroom set-up, had restless nights thinking about our first-week activities, and lost track of time while engaged in conversation with likeminded friends and colleagues on how to tweak and improve our instruction for students.

Twitter, Pinterest, and Teachers Pay Teachers are filled to brim with cutesy, kitschy back-to-school worksheets, as well as games and activities, all designed to get to know students. These games, strategies, and activities are fun; they foster communication, cooperation, and collaboration. They can be critical during those initial days when we are establishing community and developing routines, not an easy feat when our students still smell of chlorine, sand continues to cling to their sandals, and early wake-ups bring all of us into the classroom bleary-eyed. Using these activities, we get to know our students and they get to know each other—likes and dislikes, interests and experiences. Our interactions with our students are driven by our desire to know who they are, where they come from, what makes them tick. These connections build relationships fundamental to developing a classroom community.

If our goal in those early days is to also launch a writing community, then at the beginning of the school year we must create specific experiences and events that will allow that to occur as well. We must establish at the outset that one of the foundational blocks of our classroom community is that we are writers. A robust writing community will not automatically emerge merely because we are in a language arts classroom. It does not just magically happen; we cannot wish it into being. It's not as simple as providing pencils, paper, and writing prompts. A writing community will develop and grow only if we carve out the precious time to make it happen and put forth the effort and energy into bringing it to fruition.

> *Anne*
>
> As I have been single for a number of years, my dear friends signed me up on a dating app and, unbeknownst to me, created a dating profile on my behalf. The information my friends were asked to fill in on the site was no secret, just stuff that most people already know about me: height, astrological sign, education, activity level, frequency of drinking/smoking, pets, and religion. Nothing really deep and confidential. The questions in the preliminary survey are easy to answer, present low risk, and allow potential daters to get an initial impression quickly. Their purpose is to enable participants to efficiently determine if there are any similarities, connections, and deal breakers—all before swiping left or right.

When students enter our classroom, we want them to have opportunities to share tidbits of information about themselves and make initial connections with each other. People Bingo, Never Have I Ever, and Would You Rather… are just some of the tried and true getting-to-know-each-other activities that we use those first hours/days to create the conditions for collegiality. But maybe you're like Anne who, when interacting with dating prospects, is eager to know more sooner rather than later. To discover more personal information about someone requires an investment of time and a willingness on the part of both individuals to be open. It involves a risk, and requires both parties to put themselves out there, to be transparent and vulnerable. You may be sitting back reading this thinking, "I don't care that much about Anne's love life. I thought this was a book about writing." It is, we promise. But this anecdote illustrates the challenge that writing can pose in classrooms. When we ask students to take a risk and share personal stories, experiences, and tales from their life, we are asking them to walk into a place of openness and visibility. This can sometimes lead to discomfort, uncertainty, and anxiousness, but is often where the best writing comes from. Our lives are the impetus for rich writing, meaningful writing, powerful writing. These are the life stories that only an individual can tell and write. As Deborah Wiles stated in her interview with John Schu (2019),

> We need every person's story told—dance it, sing it, paint it, draw it, tell it, write it—in order to make up the whole of who we are. It's all story. This is why the storytellers are so important to our world and existence. And every single one of us is a storyteller.

Writing Triage

As writing teachers, we consider it our duty, responsibility, and obligation to create safe writing spaces: places where our students can tap into their lives and know that their ideas and experiences have value; an atmosphere in which they are willing to put themselves on paper and, above all, know that their story will be received with the love, care, and respect it deserves. This requires a caring community. But before we can go there, we need to start with the straightforward, low-risk questions to triage our students as writers.

Our students come to us with varied histories, as much a product of their pasts as we are of our own. When looking at your class list before the start of school, you will likely have some knowledge of your students: actors in the school show, members of the recycling team, those you know from previous encounters in the schoolyard. But we bet you probably don't know them as writers. You don't know the student who spent the summer detailing their daily adventures in a journal, or the one who wrote emails back and forth with a grandparent, or which one wrote a story fashioned after the work of their favorite author. At the same time, you probably aren't aware of the students who have not picked up a pen or pencil all summer and don't see themselves as writers, or the student who has grown up in a writing desert. Those first weeks of the new school year are the perfect time to triage your class, just like a hospital emergency room does with patients. We want to create the conditions to quickly and efficiently uncover who is *developing* as a writer? Who is *reluctant*? Who is *prolific*? To identify them in their writing journey, you need to know your student writers. Just as we intentionally invest time and energy into allowing our students to know us as writers in those early days, we need to carve out time to build the connections that will allow *us* to get to know *them*.

If you've used the Teacher-as-a-Writer activity on page 26, you know about co-constructing with your students a chart about their teacher as a writer. Imagine being able to construct a similar chart for each of your students over the course of the year. This is your goal. You want to know each of your students intimately as a writer. Consider knowing the following about each of your students:

- Preferences: formats they like to write, topics they enjoy writing about, tools they prefer to use, favorite writers they emulate
- Habits: where they like to write, when they like to write, what their writing routines are, who they enjoy sharing their writing with
- Behaviors: brainstorming techniques, planning strategies, process for writing (e.g., rehearsing strategies: daydreaming, thinking, jotting, drawing, using a graphic organizer)
- Writing History: writing life from the previous school year, writing habits at home, general feelings toward writing, commitment level to writing

Having this knowledge about a student is invaluable in planning instructional moves, determining next steps, forming groups, purposefully selecting mentor texts for writing, and informing feedback techniques and conferencing strategies, as well as in communicating strengths and areas of needs with parents.

Interest Inventory

At the beginning of the year it is informative and enlightening to sit down with each of our students and learn more about their preferences, interests, and hobbies; however, often we don't have the luxury of that much time to spend. Interest inventories enable you to maximize the amount of personal information you can get about students in a minimal amount of class time. You will gain invaluable insights into the personality and preferences of each of your students from just a few questions. For example, Tarek is a sports addict—you name it, he plays it; Mariam is fascinated with the Medieval time period she learned about in Grade 4; Olivia would live with her ear buds in listening to music all day if she could; Nolan's passion for the environment is clear by his participation in the school Recycling Team, Environment Club, and volunteerism at the local conservation

---

Students will
- reflect on their preferences, interests, and hobbies

Teacher will
- begin to craft a writer profile for each student based on interests and hobbies
- be able to support students in identifying their writing territories (e.g., ideas and writing formats)

authority. All these tidbits of information allow you to make immediate connections with your students and to identify patterns and trends between classmates. Interest inventories are a low-risk way to get students to dig into their own lives for potential writing territories they might never have considered. Tarek could use his extensive background knowledge and passion for sport as ideas for potential writing: an article about his favorite athlete, a descriptive poem highlighting the exhilaration of a three-point shot, or a short story detailing the championship game.

As teachers, let's show our students how to use their interests as a source for writing. Take a topic of interest and start unravelling its vast potential for writing territories. Consider creating and personalizing your own interest inventory to meet the needs of your grade and students.

See page 45 for an Interest Inventory adapted from the work of Steven Layne and Donalyn Miller.

Writing Survey

A writing survey is the second step in creating a complete picture of each student as a writer. Carefully selected questions provide invaluable information regarding writing preferences, habits, and the writing history of your students. Pointed and thoughtful questionnaires provide an immense amount of information to support you in triaging your class as writers. Writing surveys

- enable you to get a general sense of your class's attitude toward writing
- help you make informed instructional decisions for writing mini-lessons
- serve as the basis for your initial writing conferences with students

Students will
- *reflect on their writing preferences, habits, writing history, and attitude*

Teacher will
- *begin to craft a writer profile for each student based on the information provided*
- *be able to support students in identifying their writing territories (i.e., ideas and writing formats)*

As part of the writing triage, a writing survey is the equivalent of a diagnostic assessment, so it's important to consider how you will deliver and administer this task to students. Students need to know that honesty is imperative: you value their thoughts, ideas, and opinions, and do not want them to censor themselves. As a result, we strongly encourage you administer it over a week, rather than rushing through in one day. By reading and talking out each question together, you will support your students in slowing down their thinking to respond thoughtfully. For example, on the Writing Survey on page 47, question 11 asks students to identify what behaviors describe them as a writer; you might administer it this way:

See page 47 for a Writing Survey.

> *Take a moment to think back on the writing you have done in previous years. I wonder: Do you like to talk about your ideas before you write? Some people really benefit from having a chance to chat with a trusted friend as they tease out ideas before they are expected to put pencil to paper. Other people like to sit quietly alone with their own thoughts and even make lists in a notebook, on sticky notes, or sometimes on a graphic organizer. I wonder what you like to do.*

By encouraging students to reflect and then respond honestly, we convey to them that this is a judgment-free zone where their authentic responses are valued and desired.

Imagine giving students the same survey at the end of the year, after their experiences as writers in your class. This is a phenomenal way to celebrate student growth, accomplishments, and successes.

I Am a Writer Who…

If you're like us, by the Friday of the first week of school your feet are killing you; it's the first time your feet have been in shoes in months and you've got the blisters to prove it. You're taking Tylenol to alleviate the pain in your back from

Students will
- begin to recognize their own writing habits, characteristics, and preferences

Teacher will
- begin to craft a writer profile for each student based on the information provided

standing all day. And your medium coffee has now morphed into an XL just to keep the yawns at bay. All you can think about is what take-out food you're picking up on the way home and which Netflix show you are going to fall asleep to on the couch. The week has been a whirlwind of activity, centred on getting to know each other better. When focusing on building our writing community we need to go further. We must begin to explore ourselves and each other as writers. The creation of an I Am a Writer Who… list poem will support students in recognizing that they have developed as writers over time and have personal writing habits and preferences.

1. Use question stems for classroom discussion and to support students in thinking about themselves as writers:
   - Where do you like to write?
   - What topics do you like to write about?
   - Where do you get ideas for your writing?
   - Who inspires you as a writer?
   - What do you need as a writer to be successful?
   - What are your favorite genres/formats to write?

2. Post these questions on charts around the room.
3. On each chart, model your own thinking to help students get started.
4. Students can travel in small groups to think, talk, and graffiti their own ideas on each chart.
5. Follow this brainstorming activity with a conversation that highlights trends, identifies connections, and notes any *aha!*s that pop off the page.
6. This information can be used by the writing community (including you) to create personal I Am a Writer Who… list poems. Copy and distribute the I Am a Writer template from page 50. Ensure that student responses are varied and address a number of the question stems posed. Encourage students to complete each sentence stem truthfully. Consider conferencing with each writer to review their completed poem and discuss the ideas shared.
7. Display edited poems prominently in the classroom with an accompanying photo of each writer.

We are always amazed at the level of candor and transparency that our students put forth in their poems. These revelations enable us to quickly get to know our students as unique individual writers, as well as to uncover trends in our classroom. Their straightforward, honest responses signal to us that they already are placing trust in our writing community.

Student Sample: Janay's I Am a Writer poem

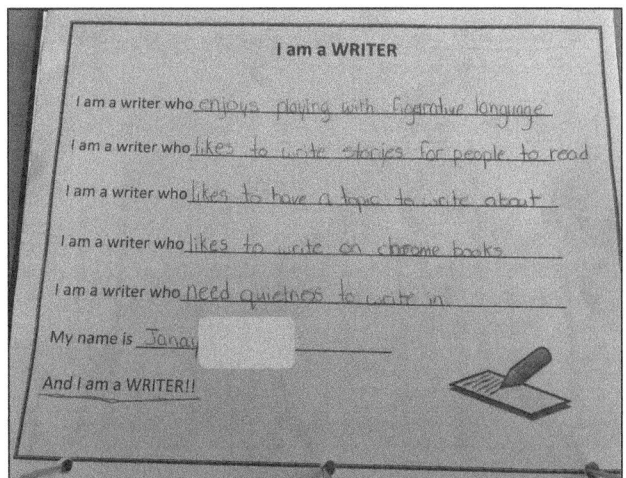

Extension

Consider having your students create I Am a Writer Who… poems multiple times throughout the year. This activity enables students to document, track, and recognize their growth and development as writers over time. The awareness that they have improved and changed motivates students to continue on their writing journey. At the same time, it provides us with invaluable information on our writers.

The Writer's Notebook

Countless authors have spoken about the worth and purpose of writer's notebooks to their writing lives. Ralph Fletcher states,

> Keeping a notebook is the single best way I know to survive as a writer. It encourages you to pay attention to your world, inside and out. It serves as a container to keep together all the seeds you gather until you're ready to plant them. It gives you a quiet place to catch your breath and begin to write. (Fletcher, 1996, p. 1)

For us, notebooks are a place where ideas are gathered, seeds are planted, drafts are begun, writing is tinkered with, craft is explored, and short pieces are launched. Whether leather-bound, a spiral notebook, or a book-store journal, a writer's notebook becomes an essential, treasured tool for a writer. This organic vessel holds thoughts and ideas. It houses attempts at craft. It contains lists of favorite lines and words. Most importantly, it protects newborn ideas until they can be nourished and developed into more formal pieces.

The notebook is indispensable in the early days of school when we ask students to mine their lives for writing potential. They must have a space that safely harbors their fragile experiences, memories, feelings, and ideas. For us, writer's notebooks become *the* place writers play, draft, and preserve and accumulate ideas. It is not a diary, a place for journal responses or daily recounts. The writing activities we carefully and intentionally lead students through create the conditions for powerful writing. They take our students to places where they uncover writing territories and topics, discover their voice, and come to know that their writing has value. A reciprocal benefit is that we intimately get to know our students and can support them as writers at a much deeper level. We are able to match specific students with particular mentor texts and nudge them further into places and spaces that hold significant meaning and writing possibility. The following activities are designed with these purposes in mind.

Notebook Tour

We swear we are not Peeping Toms, but we have to admit that, when out for a nightly walk, a drive through the country, or a holiday Christmas-light tour, we love to look into windows and catch a glimpse inside the homes we are passing. These brief moments illuminate the life that exists within those four walls and we are often intrigued. Let your students experience this glimpse into your writing life by allowing them to explore your writer's notebook. Peering into your writer's notebook, students learn a variety of things about you: likes/dislikes, habits, hobbies, family, struggles/challenges, achievements/celebrations, thoughts, ideas, feelings.

Sidebar:

Donald Graves, Lucy Calkins, Linda Reif, Ralph Fletcher, and Aimee Buckner all explore the power and purpose of keeping a writer's notebook. We encourage you to check out *Living Between the Lines* by Lucy Calkins, *Breathing In, Breathing Out* and *A Writer's Notebook* by Ralph Fletcher, and *Notebook Know-How* by Aimee Buckner.

Consider investigating digital resources that provide an in-depth look at notebooks:

Sharing Our Notebooks: Learning From Notebook Keepers at http://www.sharingournotebooks.amylv.com/2020/03/keeping-notebooktogether.html

A Peek Inside My Writer's Notebook by Ruth Ayres (YouTube video) at https://www.youtube.com/watch?v=AZE3_j6a59w

Students will
- discover that their teacher keeps a writer's notebook, uses their life as a source for ideas, and writes in various forms and formats

Teacher will
- share their notebook and pieces they have written

1. Touring through the pages of your Writer's Notebook, with you as guide, permits students to learn intimate snippets about you, your life, and experiences. Be willing to open up your life to your new writing community by selecting and tagging a few pages to share. Spotlight a variety of pieces and talk about what inspired that writing:

   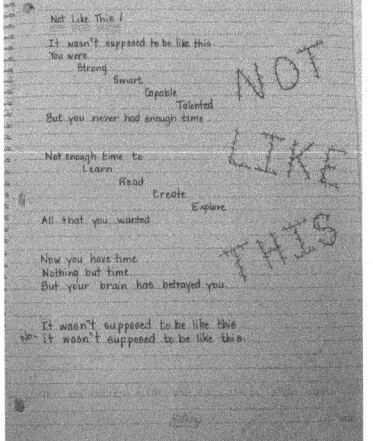

   The other day I went for a walk with my husband Peter and I was struck by the way Mother Nature was preparing for fall. In particular I was captivated by the color of leaves, the sound of the geese loudly honking their migration plans, the activity of squirrels scampering about collecting nuts. The feel of the cool breeze and the weakening sun spoke to me. All of nature's splendor seemed to awaken my senses and I couldn't wait to get home and capture my walk in words.

   Something I'd like to share about me is that my Mom is ill with Alzheimer's disease. I find myself writing about her a lot lately: memories I have about her, stories I treasure, and how angry and sad I am that she is here physically but her memories continue to disappear. I write about how I wish things could be different. It helps me cope and release the feelings and emotions pent up inside me. Here is a poem I wrote recently using the line "It wasn't supposed to be like this..."

2. Create a T-chart to record the piece of writing and its form on one side, and what students learned about you personally and as a writer on the other.

Extension

As students build their knowledge and understanding of the purpose and power of writer's notebooks, consider using the following books:
- Ralph Fletcher, *A Writers Notebook: Unlocking the Writer Within You*
- Jennifer Holm, *Middle School is Worse Than Meatloaf*
- Marissa Moss, *Amelia's Notebook*
- Kent Redeker, *Angela Anaconda: My Notebook*

Highlighting and exploring these texts is an effective way to explore notebooks with your students if you yourself do not keep one—yet!

Cover Creation

Students will
- discover that the cover of a notebook is a personal representation of the writer within

Teacher will
- share their notebook cover and talk through the images that are showcased on the front that paint a picture of the writer

In the first weeks of school, students learn countless things about their teacher. For example. Anne's students discover that she starts each day with a large coffee from Tim Hortons; she loves cinnamon gum; sour cream and onion chips are her favorite treat; her dog Roy is very mischievous; walking on the beach grounds her; she loves to read and sell books to kids; she has two nieces, Emma and Charlotte; she enjoys traveling around the world; her dad is her hero; Cape Breton Island is near and dear to her heart. These discoveries stem from conversations held with the class and off-the-cuff chats that arise spontaneously during lessons.

Since the teacher holds the floor more often than students, it's no surprise that students learn more about us than they share about themselves. It's key we flip the script and provide time and opportunities for students to share similar tidbits and snippets about themselves with our classroom community. Cover Creation allows students to do just that.

1. Collect photos, images, magazine clippings, stickers, and or words/phrases that portray you and your life. Share a number of items with students and talk about why they represent your interests, hobbies, likes, etc.

   Isn't this a spectacular picture of fall? Fall is my favorite season for many reasons. Since I grew up on a farm, this time of year signifies the end of the growing cycle and reveals the bounty of a good harvest. My birthday is on October 30 and, with Halloween just the next day, many of my childhood memories are tied to that special night. I also love the cooler temperatures, the changing leaves, and going apple picking. Wrapping myself in a sweater and boots and even curling up on the couch with a blanket is a delight this time of year. Not to mention Thanksgiving and all the delicious food and family fun. I hope you can see that this one image spawns many writing ideas and highlights a lot about me!

   Model for students how the photos and magazine clippings are rich and dense with writing potential, and provide multiple writing possibilities.
2. Demonstrate how to cut, arrange, layer, and assemble selected artifacts into an eye-catching display on a notebook cover.
3. Send home a letter informing parents of the task to select and collect significant artifacts to be used for their child's notebook cover; see sample letter on page 49. Provide a few days for the collection to be completed.
4. If you have access to and permission to use former students' Writer's Notebooks, consider color copying five or six; or you can print samples from the internet. Distribute these images to groups of students and have them consider the following questions:
   - What do you think their hobbies are?
   - What are they interested in?
   - What sort of things do you think they like?
   - What do you think they care about and value?
   - What other things can you notice/learn from the cover?
   - Based on what you see, what topics do you think might appeal to this writer?

This investigation allows fellow writers to see how the cover plays a critical role in illustrating who the author of the notebook is.
5. Once students are prepared to begin creating their covers, let the fun and mess begin. Be sure to have lots of magazines and decorative items on hand for students who might not have access to artifacts from home.

Extension

Our dear friend Cara laminates the covers in one long piece and does not cut them into individual covers until after the big reveal. Students sit in two lines facing each other on the carpet with space down the middle for the big roll out! Cara ceremoniously unfurls the roll of covers and asks each facing partnership to consider the same questions posed above. Students are excited and eager to discover interesting facts, bits, and stories about each other. Every few minutes, have students scoot along the carpet and investigate another creative cover.

Mining Our Lives for Writing Ideas

Once Writer's Notebook covers are created and celebrated for their unique design and elements, the excitement and energy in the room is palpable. However, this is often coupled with a sense of uncertainty and hesitation by students who flip nervously through, looking at the endless empty, lined, pages. They wonder: *Am I expected to fill this book? Do I have enough ideas to write about? What am I supposed to put in here? Who is going to read this? Will my writing in here be marked?* These questions all get answered in time, but it is imperative that we recognize the vulnerability of our writers and offer them support, guidance, and direction in approaching the page with a sense of confidence. First interactions with the blank pages of notebooks need to be successful writing experiences. So choose to target a topic that students are experts on—themselves!

Each person's life is unique and an endless source of inspiration. As teachers, we must carefully and intentionally model how we mine our own life as the ultimate source for writing ideas. Our lives are expansive territories from which we can find small moments to home in on and write about. With our support, direction, and modeling, our students will feel confident and capable to use their own life as a source for writing.

The following mini-lessons are essential activities that pave the way for students discovering their inner voice. From these activities, students come to know that their life is an endless fountain from which they can draw. They uncover

- things they know and are able to do
- their likes and dislikes
- memorable moments that are written on their heart
- emotionally charged experiences
- locations that evoke memories
- unforgettable people

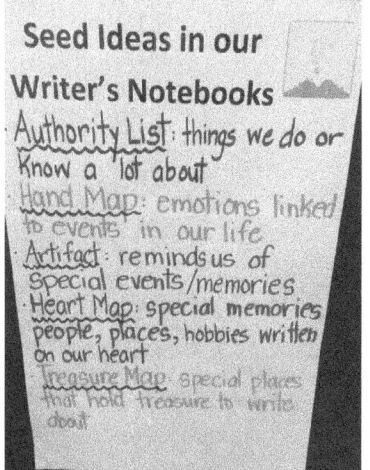

Sample Mini-Lessons from Respected Writers

Authority List

From *Teaching the Qualities of Writing* by JoAnn Portalupi and Ralph Fletcher, 2004
Purpose: To generate a list of topics that students are the authority on. These topics are things they know something about due to experiences, things they know how to do, and things they are interested in.

Love it/Loathe It

From *Marvelous Minilessons for Teaching Intermediate Writing, Grades 4–6* by Lori Jamison Rog
Purpose: To generate a list of things that elicit a strong emotional response from the writer. These potential writing topics are sources of love and angst.

Heart Map

From *Mentor Texts: Teaching Writing Through Children's Literature* by Lynne Dorfman & Rose Cappelli, 2007; *Heart Maps: Helping Students Create and Craft Authentic Writing* by Georgia Heard, 2016
Purpose: To identify mementos, topics, issues, people we care deeply and passionately about, things that truly matter and are written on our hearts.

Hand Map

From *Mentor Texts: Teaching Writing Through Children's Literature* by Lynne Dorfman & Rose Cappelli, 2007
Purpose: To discover that writing often stems from strong emotions that are linked to personal experiences.

Dig Up Buried Stories

From *Teaching the Qualities of Writing* by JoAnn Portalupi and Ralph Fletcher, 2004
Purpose: To discover that writing can stem from memories connected to a special place.

Writing Bingo

From *The Write Genre* by Lori Jamison Rog and Paul Kropp, 2004
Purpose: To generate a variety of potential writing ideas based on juicy prompts.

Unforgettable People and Pets

Purpose: To generate a list of people and pets that stand out in our mind and/or heart.

Possible Mentor Texts:
Barbara Abercrombie, *Charlie Anderson* (Pets)
Joseph Coelho, *Grandpa's Stories* (Family)
Arthur Dorros, *Abuela* (Family)
Bob Graham, *Rose Meets Mr. Wintergarten* (Neighbors)
Gloria Houston, *My Great-Aunt Arizona* (Family)
Jiyeon Pak, *Finding Grandma's Memories* (Family)
Margie Palatini, *The Perfect Pet* (Pets)
Roni Schotter, *Nothing Ever Happens on 90th Street* (Neighbors)
Liliana Stafford & Stephen Michael King, *Amelia Ellicott's Garden* (Neighbors)
Kathy Stinson, *Harry and Walter* (Neighbors)
Rebecca Upjohn, *Lily and the Paper Man* (People We Pass)
Judith Viorst, *The Tenth Good Thing About Barney* (Pets)
Laura Williams, *The Can Man* (People We Pass)

We are all surrounded by people every day: our families, colleagues, neighbors, friends, even the people in line at the grocery store. Our interactions can be sincere and meaningful or simply incidental, but all make an impression on us in some way. These people color our world and are a limitless source of writing inspiration.

1. Have students divide a page in their writer's notebook into four equal sections.
2. For each section, provide students with a prompt to generate ideas of people. Box 1 is for Family:

   The people who are always there for you, cheering you on, bringing a smile to your face, and/or making you laugh out loud. You know, the grandparent who never misses a game or recital, the aunt who shares your passion for reading, or the cousin you look forward to playing with at family gatherings.

3. Have students take a moment to jot down a few names.
4. In subsequent boxes consider having students generate ideas from the following prompts.

Box 2: Neighbors

Noisy, kind, helpful, intimidating, interesting, quirky, generous.

Anne

I fondly remember trick or treating each year, and the freshly baked peanut butter cookies that Mr. and Mrs. Dale ceremoniously removed from the cookie sheet and gently placed in a baggie for me. We would devour those mouth-watering morsels as soon as we got into the car.

Box 3: Pets

Dogs, cats, fish, guinea pigs, reptiles, bunnies—who hasn't longed for a pet? Lucky are those who actually get one and don't have to make do with loving a friend's pet from afar.

Mary

I will never forget the day my husband Peter indulged our daughter's constant yearning for a puppy without so much as a phone call home to ask my opinion. This bundle of fur magically appeared in the backyard, followed by Jennifer bursting in the door, exclaiming, "Daddy bought me a puppy!!!" I felt confusion and astonishment as I attempted to make eye contact with Peter, who was clearly averting my gaze.

Mining Our Lives for Writing Ideas

Box 4: Mentors

Who are coaches, instructors, teachers who stand out in your mind? Maybe have taught you an invaluable skill, pushed you to try your best, or provided you with discipline when you needed it. They are people who have made a difference in your life.

> ### Anne
> I cherish my memories of my 4H leader Jessie Beattie. Her kindness, expansive knowledge, patience, dedication to youth, and warm nature instilled in me a will to be a better person in my community. At the same time, my piano teacher Mrs. Mayo was frequently frustrated by my lack of commitment to practicing my scales and pieces. She toiled endlessly to try to change me, but to no avail.

5. Have students share with an elbow partner one person or pet and the accompanying story.

Destination Known/Unknown

Purpose: To generate a list of places students have been to or long to visit.

Possible Mentor Texts:
Linda Bailey, *Carson Crosses Canada*
Jo Ellen Bogart, *Gifts*
Natalia Diaz, *A Ticket Around the World*
Lonely Planet Travel Books for Kids
Lynne Rae Perkins, *Pictures From Our Vacation*
Miroslav Sasek, *This is the World*
Pat Shewchuk, *In Lucia's Neighborhood*
Sarah Stewart, *The Gardener*

We love to explore our local community, our country, and the world at large. Like the Ontario licence plate slogan *Yours to discover*, we want our students to come to know that their neighborhood, community, city, country, and world are all sources of writing potential.

1. On the Destination Known/Unknown template on page 51, show students that the centre represents the location closest to where they live (i.e., neighborhood) and subsequent circles moving outward represent increasing distances from their home: community, city, country, world.
2. In the innermost circle, model for students how to generate places in their neighborhood they enjoy going to and are linked to a memory; e.g., local park, hockey arena, skate park, local diner, variety store, etc.
3. Have students generate ideas for other destinations. Whether students have first-hand knowledge and experience traveling to a particular destination or need time to investigate and research a dream location, writing about a place opens up a world of endless landscapes and adventures.
4. Once students have generated ideas for each circle, have them share some of the locales and tell the class about an adventure they had there or an adventure they dream of having.

> ### Mary
> I had the opportunity to visit the house that was the inspiration for Green Gables in Lucy Maud Montgomery's *Anne of Green Gables*. While I was there, I took the time to stroll along Lovers' Lane and the Haunted Wood Trail, places I had only read about in Montgomery's books. I hope to return again to the Maritimes to travel the coastal highway of Nova Scotia, visiting the many lighthouses that dot the landscape.

> ### Writers in the House
>
> Stories trigger memories. They draw us in and compel us to reminisce about our own personal experiences. The story connects the writer and reader in a profound and intimate way. As teachers, we can stage these opportunities by selecting text that will stimulate connection and recollection, books that inspire students to write in the style and pattern of the author and serve as fodder for personal writing ideas. Since we can't physically bring an actual writer into the room each day, we do the next best thing by bringing authors' art into the room in the form of their books. Just as we model exemplary reading to students each day, we must set out to do the same with excellent writing. We highlight quality text for students to use as mentors for their own pieces.
>
> Based on his meta-analysis of reading research, Steven Krashen informs us that "Writing style does not come from actual writing experience, but from reading." (Krashen, 2004, p. 132) So let's ensure that our students are reading text that is chock full of writing potential. Inspect your classroom collection or the library to find titles that can be used as a springboard for student writing. The lessons that follow were fashioned after interacting with exceptional pieces of writing. When read aloud to students, these phenomenal texts spark endless reaction, response, and ideas for personal writing. They are tried and true—always successful writing experiences for students.

Adapted from *6 + 1 Traits of Writing* by Ruth Culham, 2005
Purpose: To use treasured artifacts as a stimulus for writing

Possible Mentor Texts:
Eve Bunting, *The Memory String*
Paul Fleischman, *The Matchbox Diary*
Mem Fox, *Wilfrid Gordon McDonald Partridge*
Anne Louise MacDonald, *The Memory Stone*

Mining a Memento

In many long-term care homes, outside each room you will find a glass case that holds the resident's treasured mementos. Photos, figurines, medals, badges, documents, ball caps, and model vehicles adorn the shelf. These keepsakes serve as a reminder of the resident's life and even support dementia patients in identifying their room when disorientated. These items hold little monetary value to others, but to the owner are priceless. Is it any wonder that we, too, have drawers filled with notes, ticket stubs, buttons, stones, medals, shells, coins, etc. that transport us back to magical moments in our own lives? So let's start mining our mementos for memories.

1. Gather an assortment of objects you have collected over time. Select items that you treasure and that your students will be able to relate to and connect with. It may be something a dear family member gave you, a special item you purchased on holiday, or an item from nature that reminds you of where and when you discovered it. Good examples are a concert ticket stub, a letter from a relative, a shell from a beach holiday, a medal from a competition. Place these mementos in a basket or box and bring them into class to share.
2. Read aloud one of the picture books listed as mentor texts. Be sure to stop periodically to draw students' attention to how the various objects in the story evoke specific memories for the characters:

> She held the warm egg and told Wilfrid Gordon about the tiny speckled blue eggs she had once found in a bird's nest in her aunt's garden.

> She put a shell to her ear and remembered going to her beach by tram long ago and how hot she had felt in her button-up boots.
> —from *Wilfrid Gordon MacDonald Partridge* by Mem Fox

3. Take a few minutes to reveal each object you have brought to class and offer an explanation as to why you treasure it dearly:

    Take a look at this button I received when I went to Walt Disney World in Florida a number of years ago. As soon as I hold it I am transported back to the moment we entered the gates and were each ceremoniously given a button. My nieces were vibrating with excitement and anticipation. Their smiles lit up their faces and, to this day, I can close my eyes and hear their giggles and squeals in my mind.

4. Encourage students to search their own homes for a personal memento. Consider sending home a letter to families explaining the guidelines for this activity.
5. Once students return to school with their treasured object, have them share in groups their item and the thoughts, emotions, and stories connected to it.
6. After sharing, we recommend you take a photo of each artifact. The print of the photo can be then glued into each student's writer's notebook as a permanent keepsake.
7. Consider having students create a web around the image that details their object, where and when they received it, and why is important.

I Am From

Adapted from
Leap Into Literacy by Kathy Gould Lundy, 2007, pp 104–105
Purpose: To investigate various places, people, relationships, food, celebrations, and sayings that have shaped us into who we are.

Mentor Text: *Where I'm From* by George Ella Lyon
A Google search will lead you to sites that feature this timeless poem.

We've all heard the phrase "You are one of a kind"—and each of us truly is! Our food preferences, favorite hobbies, keepsakes, and family traditions all unite to make us who we are. They speak to our personality and what matters most to us. This lesson enables students to search within themselves for their unique attributes, habits, and pleasures, and to bring them onto the page in a powerful poem.

"Where I'm From" by George Ella Lyon is a poignant poem that can be used as a shared reading over multiple days or as a read aloud. The text should be revisited to build familiarity and a sense of appreciation for the authenticity and nuances of the writing. Kathy Gould Lundy (2007) offers a very structured procedure to have students create their own genuine poem based on "Where I'm From" which we have adapted here:

1. Guide students through a series of prompts to generate ideas. Suggested prompts:
   - What food is guaranteed to make your mouth water?
   - When you're on your way to school, what do you see?
   - What phrases and expressions do your family use a lot?
   - Do you have a special toy/object/gift that you cherish? Where do you store this treasure?
   - Is there an unforgettable place you would love to see again? Name it.
   - What is your favorite holiday? Describe all the things that make it special to you.
   - Some people are so close to you, it's like they are written on your heart. Name one or two of these people and explain why they have touched your heart and left a mark.

2. As you share each prompt, take time to model what a quality descriptive response looks like and sounds like, including using the stem *I am from* in the response:

   What food is guaranteed to make your mouth water?

   I am from Dairy Queen's Pecan Mudslide soft-serve ice cream treat erupting with hot fudge, gooey caramel, and salty pecans.

3. Be sure to provide students with ample time to play around with word choice, phrasing, and stanza order to arrive at a finished piece that sounds good to their ear and heart.
4. Have students share their I Am From poems with a partner and elaborate on what each line means.

Extensions

1. Students create a video presentation of their I Am From poem. Pairing carefully selected images and photos with their recorded voice enhances the presentation and impact of their personal poem.
2. Have students use artifacts that represent them to form the letters of the title *I Am From*: paint brushes, medals, coins, books, pens, chocolate bars, pucks, pointe shoes. Students use personal and thoughtful items to represent themselves and to enrich the presentation of their piece.

When I Was Young

Purpose: To investigate memories linked to our home, neighborhood, and community.

Mentor Text: *When I Was Young in the Mountains* by Cynthia Rylant

The recesses of our mind hold memories we savor. They remind us of where we have been and the experiences that have shaped us. These little nuggets and small moments pack a punch and are utterly priceless to us. Having students travel down memory lane enables them to revisit these memories and honor them in their writing.

1. Read aloud *When I Was Young in the Mountains* by Cynthia Rylant. Be sure to stop periodically to draw student's attention to how the language and word choice appeals to all the reader's senses and creates beautiful mind pictures.
2. After you have read aloud the text, encourage students to reflect on a place that is near and dear to their hearts; for example, a cottage or campground, a park or conservation area, homes of relatives or friends, the local hockey arena or community centre.
3. Ask students to write a few significant memories associated with that particular place using the sentence stem *When I was young…*

Student sample: Luke, Grade 6

> *When I was young in Lambeth I loved to go hiking in the forest behind my Grandparent's house with them and my brother and sister. We never had a particular destination in mind, we would just turn around whenever we were tired. My favorite hikes took place in winter on cold crisp days when there was a blanket of snow on the ground. I loved seeing the animal tracks in the snow. We would hike around fallen trees, over old farm fences, and through tall grass. My grandpa would bring his special hockey stick without the blade in case of coyotes. When we returned to the warm house if you were lucky we were able to sneak my grandma's amazing chocolate chip peanut butter balls into your mouth.*

If You're Not From…

Purpose: To consider how the unique features of our families and/or school impacts our daily lives.

Mentor Text: *If You're Not From the Prairie* by David Bouchard

David Bouchard skilfully and beautifully explores how the unique features of a region effects an individual's daily life. We have taken the liberty of adapting his text to investigate the influence family and school have on a student's life and memories.

1. Read aloud the text *If You're Not From the Prairie* by David Bouchard. Draw students' attention to the repetition of phrases and how the writing celebrates the joys of living in such a distinct environment.
2. Ask students to consider their own environment and write a stanza about harsh winters, high winds, humid summers, or ice in the harbor as a quick write.
3. Once students are familiar with the format and structure of the piece, invite them to write a few stanzas about their school and/or family.

Student sample: Cooper, Grade 6

If you're not from the Kelly family
You don't know cat hair.
You can't know cat hair.
The grey magnetic black fabric-seeking hair will do you no harm
But it will cling to almost anything you don't want it to.
Wherever you travel it is always there to remind you of who you left at home.
If you're not from the Kelly family
You don't know cat hair.

4. Have students share their drafts with peers to build your writing community.
5. Provide students time and opportunity to revise their writing. Draw their attention to one or two writing traits—word choice, phrasing, appeal to senses, organization—to enhance their polished piece.

Operation Notebook Investigation

While students are mining their lives for writing territories we are taking as many opportunities as we can to explore their notebooks. We curl up with them, pore over their work, and track the themes and patterns that emerge from their writing. We strive to learn as much as we can about them from the scratches and marks their pens leave behind on the page. We discover who they are, the experiences that shape them, the people they hold dear, the places that matter, and the things they are passionate and knowledgeable about. The tasks explored in this chapter enable us to support, guide, and teach students how to find their voice, express their thoughts, and generate topics that are meaningful to them. When students see their voices are welcomed, respected, and heard, they know that they are cherished members of our writing community.

Interest Inventory

Name: _____

1. What do you enjoying doing in your free time?

2. Do you belong to any clubs or teams at school? If so, what are they?

3. Do you belong to any clubs or teams outside of school? If so, what are they?

4. What kind of movies do you like?

5. What are your favorite TV shows?

6. Are you a fan of any professional sports? (e.g., NHL, MLB, NFL, PGA, MLS, etc.)

7. What music do you enjoy? (favorite kind of music/musician/group)

8. If you could have three wishes granted, what would they be?

9. If you were able to time travel, what time and place would you chose?

Interest Inventory (cont'd)

10. If you had the chance to meet any person, living or dead, who would it be?

11. If you could pick any three books from a bookstore for free, what would they be?

13. If you could go on a trip to any place in the world today, where would you go?

Circle anything on the list you would like to know more about.

crafts	poetry	jokes
construction	theatre	magic
electronics	cars	sports
famous people	animals	drawing
music	insects	writing
woodwork	science	trains
history	dancing	aliens
foreign lands	singers	travel
printing	planes	health
art	detectives	conservation
electricity	outer space	experiments
monsters	cooking	

Writing Survey

Name: _____

Please complete your responses honestly and accurately. The information you share will help me to get to know you as a writer.

1. If you had a chance to write every day or not, would you? ☐ Yes ☐ No

2. Why do you write?

3. Where do you like to write?

4. Do you choose to write in your spare time? ☐ Yes ☐ No

5. Who do you share your writing with?

6. How do you feel about sharing your writing with others?

7. How do you find topics for your writing?
   - ☐ assigned by teacher
   - ☐ experiences I've had
   - ☐ my imagination
   - ☐ things I have learned
   - ☐ from books
   - ☐ places I've visited
   - ☐ questions I have
   - ☐ things I love
   - ☐ from movies/TV shows
   - ☐ things I've seen
   - ☐ things I know a lot about
   - ☐ things I want to change

8. What do you enjoy writing about?

9. What kinds of writing do you do at home or at school? (for example: letters, stories, journal entries, reports, comics, poems, etc.) Put a star beside your favorite.

10. What writing tools do like to use? (for example: a journal, blank paper, lined paper, writer's notebook, pencils, pens, markers, etc.)

Writing Survey (cont'd)

11. What statements describe you as a writer?

I like to talk about my ideas before I write.	☐ Usually	☐ Sometimes	☐ Never
I make a list of my ideas before I write.	☐ Usually	☐ Sometimes	☐ Never
I like to sketch and draw prior to writing.	☐ Usually	☐ Sometimes	☐ Never
I choose to think quietly to myself before writing.	☐ Usually	☐ Sometimes	☐ Never

12. When drafting, do stop and read over what you have written?   ☐ Yes   ☐ No

13. What craft techniques do you use most often in your writing? (for example: metaphor/simile, magic of three, repetition, alliteration, personification, proper nouns, using quotes, etc.)

14. Circle the number that represents how you feel about writing.

    ```
    1          2          3          4          5
    YUCK!                                    LOVE IT!
    ```

15. Do you find any of these things challenging? Check all that apply.
    - ☐ finding an idea
    - ☐ growing/expanding ideas
    - ☐ completing a piece
    - ☐ assigned writing
    - ☐ revising your writing
    - ☐ spelling
    - ☐ punctuation
    - ☐ handwriting

16. What do you think would make you a better writer?

17. Tell me about a piece of writing you have done that you are proud of.

18. What are your strengths as a writer?

19. What is your writing goal this year?

20. What else do I need to know about you as a writer?

Sample Letter: Writer's Notebook

Dear Parents,

This past week students were excited to learn that they will be receiving their own personal Writer's Notebook. This valuable resource will be a sacred place to hold writing ideas and drafts that will grow into larger writing pieces, some of which we will take to publication. Together we have viewed and explored different notebook cover samples for inspiration.

Students are invited in class to decorate and personalize the front of their Writer's Notebook in a collage format. To do this, they are asked to gather the following items this weekend to be prepared for the class activity:
- photos of family, pets, vacations, etc.
- magazine clippings that speak to them
- stickers
- words that express thoughts/opinions/ideas
- pictures or clip art of favorite activities or hobbies

Please send in only those items that your child is permitted to cut up and paste onto their notebook.

Please send these items in with you child on _____ in a labeled resealable bag. Your assistance and support is greatly appreciated!

Sincerely,

I Am a Writer

Name: _____

I am a writer who _____

I am a writer who _____

I am a writer who _____

I am a writer who _____

I am a writer who _____

My name is _____

And I am a WRITER!

Destination Known/Unknown

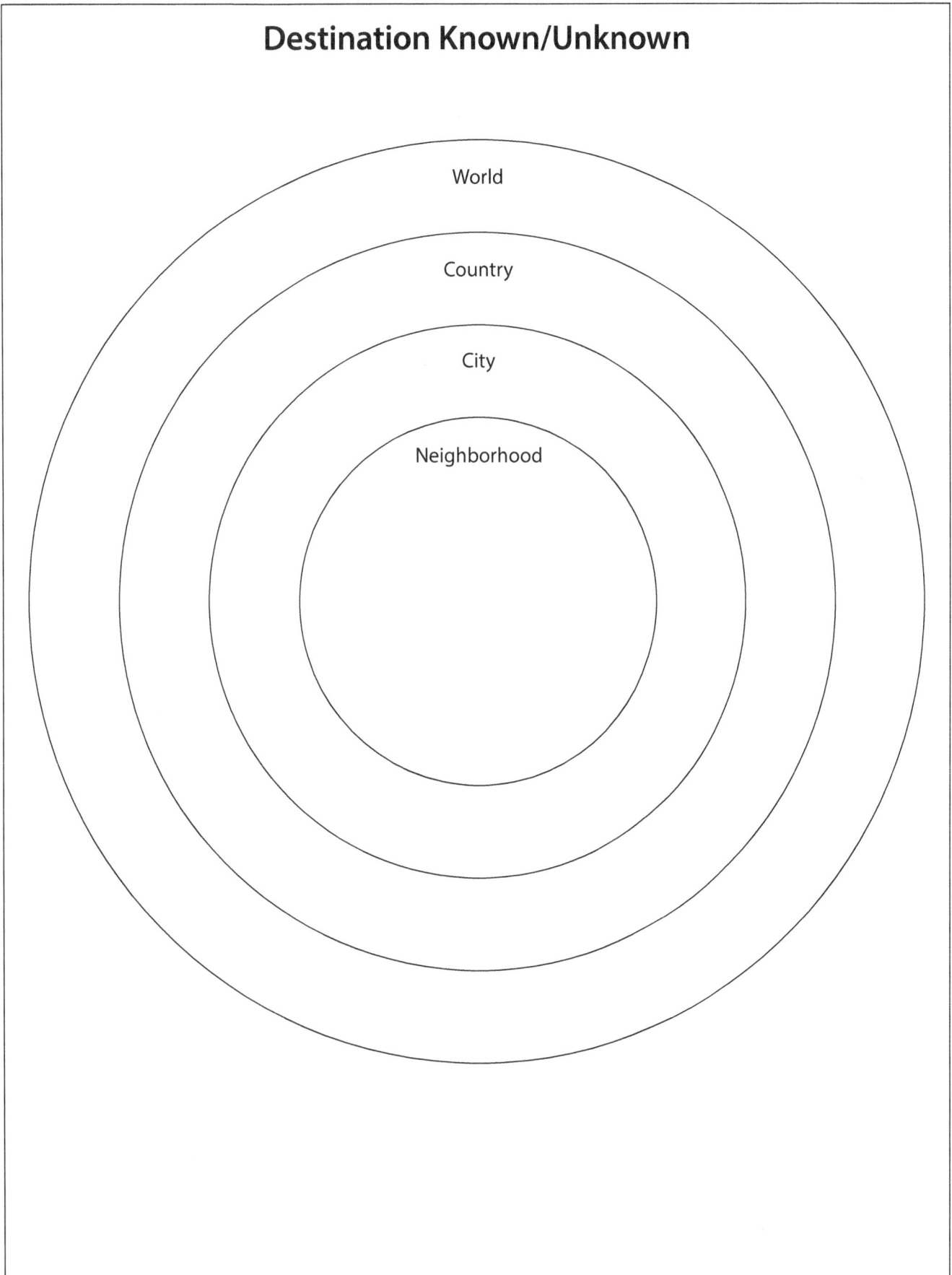

4

Third Step: Model the Habits of a Writer

We are all creatures of habit. You likely have a morning routine based on acts and behaviors that allow you to start your day on the right foot. Planning ahead sets us up for a successful start to the day. As Anne's custodian Bernie Leatherland is known to say, "Proper planning prevents poor performance." And it certainly does!

When we examine the habits of athletes, musicians, artists, hobby enthusiasts, and gardeners we find that there are distinct similarities. They each plan, find, act, and set goals for their chosen endeavor. The habits of individuals who have the desire and will to engage in a particular activity are one in the same. To become wilful writers, our students need opportunities to develop the habits of a writer in an environment that supports them. When we intentionally reveal the habits of passionate writers, our emergent authors find their voice through worthwhile idea-generation (Finding); they come to know the vast variety of forms and formats they can choose to write in and the defining features of each (Planning); they toil within a community that sustains them through reading, thinking, talking, and sharing (Acting); and they identify and strive to reach goals that will keep them developing their craft (Setting Goals). Learning and living the habits of a writer sets our students up to be capable, competent, and proficient writers. Experiencing this satisfaction and success, they come to see themselves as authors and their passion for writing flourishes. Nurturing proficiency and passion is our goal for our students.

Wilful Habits

We can't have a conversation about the habits of writers without acknowledging the pivotal work of numerous literacy leaders and authors. Graves, Murray, Calkins, Fletcher, Laminack, and Lamott have written and spoken extensively about developing a writing life. Their work influenced the daily decisions we made as teachers in developing our writing community and we have translated their thinking into the essential habits of a writer.

- Wilful writers **find** ideas to develop. Passionate writers are like detectives in their ability to sense which topics and ideas have potential. They have a heightened sense of awareness and keenly take in their surroundings. Being mindful of their writing territories, they use topics they know about, care about, and or wonder about as sources for their writing.
- Wilful writers **plan**. They consider all the different formats of text and determine which one best suits their purpose and audience. They come to know which text types they enjoy playing with and frequently explore its features and characteristics to deliver their message in a personal and unique way. They know the tools they like to use when writing. They dedicate specific times in their day for writing to develop stamina, and have their favorite spaces and places at school and home to write.
- Wilful writers **act** in specific ways. They think about their writing. We hear them talking fervently about their work. They enjoy sharing their writing with their community, friends, and family.
- Wilful writers **set goals**. As we support young writers in developing their writing skills and will, it is imperative that we guide them in setting appropriate, specific, and manageable goals that propel them as writers to new heights.

It is vital that we, as teachers, truly accept our responsibility to model and teach the habits that develop a passionate and capable writer. The habits look straightforward: Find, Plan, Act, Set Goals. But don't be fooled by their seeming simplicity. Developing entrenched and instinctive writing habits takes time, effort, and energy on behalf of the teacher in modeling these habits and on behalf of students in adopting them. We've heard it said that, while motivation gets you started, it's habit that keeps you going. This means we need to do intentional things to blatantly model, fully develop, and continue to grow writing habits in our students. It is not enough to merely identify the practices of a writer and expect students to emulate them. It is crucial that we provide our learners with regular and continual opportunities to recognize, cultivate, and internalize these actions.

Celebrating Commitment

Students will
- begin to recognize that developing a habit requires commitment, dedication, and intentionality

An effective way to explore the habits that committed and dedicated individuals exhibit is to spotlight a person of interest for your students; for example, an athlete, singer, dancer, or musician. Deconstruct the habits that have contributed to that person's skill development and success. Point out that accomplished and fulfilled readers and writers exhibit similar habits. When attempting to illustrate that developing a habit requires commitment, dedication, and intentionality, Canadian teachers often use a hockey hero as a hook. Every Saturday night many Canadian homes are glued to the TV, watching Hockey Night in Canada. Children of all ages and genders watch their heroes take to the ice and wow us with their tremendous skill and ability. But do students realize that these athletes didn't just arrive at the arena the first time, strap on their skates, hit the ice, and excel at the game? Do they know that countless hours each and every week, on and off the ice, have been dedicated to prepare for the game? Well, let's make them aware. Let's show them.

1. Select an individual that your students know, are interested in, and admire. Remember those interest inventories—did you notice a common interest among your students? Consider that as the perfect place to search out a

personality. Print a photograph of that individual and mount it in the centre of a piece of chart paper.
2. Begin by asking students to consider: How do you think this person plans for the main event (game, show, performance)? What do they do to prepare? How do they ensure they are ready? Have students brainstorm or share ideas and record them on the chart.

> *Anne*
>
> In my hockey-obsessed classroom, we investigated Sid the Kid. I guided students to think about Sidney Crosby's
> - practice schedule
> - workout routine
> - diet
> - equipment
> - participation in team meetings
> - review of game footage

3. Paying attention to a "successful" individual is meant to elicit the intentional ways in which they plan what they're going to do, when they're going to do it, and where; they find the appropriate materials they will require; the ways in which they act by thinking about what they're doing by talking to others about their activity and sharing their enthusiasm; and they set goals that are realistic and manageable, and yet push them to new heights.

Extensions

- Encourage students to investigate a famous person to uncover the time and energy they devote to honing their skills. Their investigation should reveal the habits that contribute to that individual's success.
- You might be able to use your own classroom as the subject for this lesson. Every class has an athlete, whether it's tae kwon do, cheerleading, soccer, or dance. Celebrate a student's commitment by asking them direct questions to reveal how they plan, find, act, and set goals. This will not only uncover the essential habits but will also develop a sense of community.

The Habit of Finding

Growing writers are on a journey of self-discovery. They are in the midst of learning their writing territories, discovering their topic preferences, and capitalizing on their strengths. They are also on a quest to find texts that open the flood gates to their own ideas. That's where we come in, to support students in knowing they have something to say and to believe in the worthiness of their voice. Their thoughts, ideas, and opinions have value and should be shared and heard.

Tapping into Our Notebooks

Most children in our part of Canada have the experience of traveling to the sugar bush imprinted on their memory. They see first-hand how maple trees are carefully tapped to release their precious juice one drip at a time into metal pails hanging from the trees. When pails are filled to the brim, the clear liquid is transferred to tanks where it is boiled down over an open flame into a sweet thick reduction. Students are shocked to discover that it takes approximately 35 to 40 litres of sap to produce 1 litre of sweet maple syrup to pour over our pancakes at breakfast. That is why maple syrup is affectionately called liquid gold.

We want students to envision their lives as the majestic maple tree, filled with sap (ideas) just waiting to be tapped. Just as the pail serves as a tool to collect the sap, students must discover a mechanism to contain and hold their precious ideas. Their writer's notebooks serve as the reservoir that holds the ideas till the writer is ready to turn on the heat and begin to coax and develop the idea into a sweet product.

Notebooks are holding tanks for countless ideas to be set free. Pages are filled with dormant bits and pieces that need to warmed, molded, and brought to life. As the lead writer in the class, you need to support students in returning to their notebooks to reflect on their ideas and to revisit ones they believe have the value and merit to be developed. This is a personal authentic writing opportunity. With this in mind, we encourage you to give your students time to tap into notebooks at least a few times a month to remember and discover their own liquid gold. Guide students to notice and note common themes, topics, and ideas that continually pop up, as these are their prime writing territories. Be sure to then provide time for them to write!

Burning Questions/Cool Ideas

> *Mary*
>
> I built a science lesson around Donald M. Silver's *One Small Square: Backyard*. I had Grade 3 students go out into the schoolyard to observe and examine closely a small plot of land. After returning to the classroom, students were asked to compile their observations into *Things We Noticed* and *Things We Wonder*. I was awestruck by the detailed observations and the thought-provoking questions younger students generated. Let's not keep these perceptive observations and inquisitive questions to the confines of science alone.

Consider displaying Burning Questions and Cool Ideas charts accessibly in a nook in your room. With sticky notes and pencils nearby, students can spontaneously jot and add their own questions and ideas to the collaborative class charts. Burning questions have included: *Why do all schools have Remembrance Day assemblies? Why do flies and bees get dopey in the fall? How do weeds get in the ground when no one plants them there? How do soft bugs protect themselves? Why do we recycle some plastics and not others?* Some cool ideas students have produced: *different ways to retrieve balls that have gone over the school-yard fence into a neighboring yard; using a space heater to dry our wet mittens; blending peanut butter and jam together into one spread; turning your backpack into a jetpack.*

As you notice ideas filling up the charts, steal a few moments to review them with the class and encourage students to record in their notebooks any ideas that speak to them as potential writing topics. Notice aloud with your students how one person's idea captivates and triggers another as a writer.

> This ongoing exercise is about activating our senses and imaginations, stimulating the ideas of others; it epitomizes how the shared nature of our writing community is fostered through talk.

Reading to Spark Writing

Our writers need to sample lots of text through reading, both texts we read aloud to them and those they self-select for independent reading. As curators of our classroom libraries, we carefully ensure that our students have access to high-quality, well-written text, and that our libraries contain a variety of topics and content to stimulate student writing.

> *Anne and Mary*
>
> After a number of students in Anne's class independently read *The Candy Shop War* by Brandon Mull, many were inspired to write fantastical stories of candy having magical powers. After purposely reading aloud *I'm in Charge of Celebrations* by Byrd Baylor, Mary proposed to students that they watch for the magical natural moments that embellish their own world. As a model, Mary proclaimed March 23 as Red Robin Day and wrote about her excitement of seeing her first spring robin.

It is always important to honor the reciprocal relationship between reading and writing. Good writers read. We know unequivocally that stories trigger memories and spark writing. Stories draw us in, compel us to reminisce about our own personal experiences, and inspire us to put pen to paper. As teachers, we can stage these idea opportunities by selecting texts that stimulate connection and recollection as fodder for personal writing ideas. So scour your shelves for stories and texts that will speak to your students' lived experiences, supporting them in generating ideas, finding topics, and discovering territories.

The Habit of Planning *What*

We must ensure that our students are aware of the full range and scope of writing formats to make decisions in their best writing interest. So let's reveal the variety of formats they can choose from and support them in being well-versed in a particular format's purpose and power.

Format Flea Market

Students will
- develop an awareness of the great number of formats in which they can write and use to communicate their ideas effectively

> *Anne*
>
> Snowbirds who travel to Florida from Canada each winter often go for the warm weather, inexpensive food, camaraderie found in trailer parks, daily golf, outlet shopping—and who can forget the fabulous flea markets! My Aunt Carmella loves to visit the weekly flea market near her mobile home in Lakeland, Florida. You just never know what you will find: knives, toolkits, flag poles, strawberries, oranges, clothing, jewelry, pots and pans, animals—the variety of items you can purchase is endless! Wandering up and down the never-ending rows of tables and exploring the unique wares is a truly remarkable experience.

Examples include board game instructions, a recipe, instructions on how to draw a cat, song lyrics, a poetic birthday card, a newspaper article, a report on endangered elephants, an email, a poster for an upcoming book fair, a class newsletter, a Zits comic, a short story, a biography of a Canadian hero, a memoir sample, a brochure for a theme park, a story board, a tourism pamphlet, a letter (thank-you, friendly, persuasive, to the editor of a newspaper), a variety of narratives (fairy tale, fable, tall tale, myth, legend), an advertisement, an infographic, a book review, a script for a readers theatre, a variety of poems (shape, list, cinquain, haiku, free verse), a selection of novels (graphic, mystery, s-f/fantasy, historical fiction, realistic fiction, info-fiction), informational texts, etc.

Students will
- develop an awareness of the great number of formats in which they read and write throughout the day

Consider taking the flea market experience into your own classroom by putting out an array of formats for students to peruse and use to develop their knowledge of the vast assortment of formats.

1. Place a piece of text on each student's desk. Ensure that you have a variety of formats represented.
2. Explain to students that they are to take a few moments to explore the room and identify various text formats at your Flea Market. They are expected to use the Format Flea-Market Finds template on page 82 to record their discoveries. Students should visit and jot down at least seven different formats.
3. Once students have had an opportunity to explore and record, have them gather as a class to share the various formats they discovered; for example:

Can you share a specific format you found? How do know this is a fable? What specific characteristics and features did you see in the text that justifies your thinking?

These conversations will provide you with valuable information about students' format knowledge: which types students are familiar with and which ones are new. Students' level of format knowledge will inform your next steps and instruction: which formats you need to dedicate more time and energy into exploring and deconstructing.

Format Tracker

Tracking a class's reading and writing encounters throughout the day enables students to become more aware of the variety of formats that they are exposed to and take in.

1. Explain to students:

Today we are going to read and write with our eyes wide open to the types of text formats we interact with. We will use a class anchor chart to record the text type/format and form.

Forms: descriptive, expository, narrative, persuasive

Descriptive: uses words with precision to produce a detailed picture appealing to the reader's senses. It may be about an object, a place, a person, a feeling, a thought.

Expository: uses and expresses information in order to explain, report, identify, compare, examine, and assess.

Narrative: communicates a story with a well-developed plot, commonly a beginning, middle, and end.

Persuasive: expresses a point of view with the purpose to convince the reader of an opinion, thought, or idea. It uses logical and emotional appeals to communicate its message.

Formats: report, how-to, instructions, newspaper article, recipe, comic, directions, letter, email, poster, infographic, poetry, picture book, persuasive letter, opinion piece, story, descriptive paragraph, brochure, storyboard, etc.

2. Throughout the school day, take a break from instruction and intentionally identify the forms and formats that you have interacted with as a class. Record them on the chart, including whether the piece was read or written. For example:

> Expository: read announcements; Expository: read messages/notes from families in planners; Expository: wrote messages back to families in planners; Narrative: read picture book for read-aloud; Descriptive: read poem for shared reading; Descriptive: modeled writing of a poetry verse; Expository: read math lesson instructions on interactive whiteboard; Expository: wrote an explanation to go with a scientific investigation; etc.

Tracking the various forms/formats you and your students have read and written will make them more aware of their daily "text diet" and the range of texts available to them to read and write.

3. Track the forms and formats over a few days to a week to provide additional information for a more complete picture of the immense variety of print we explore.

Block Party

Students will
- develop an awareness of the great number of formats in which they read and write throughout the day

> *Anne*
>
> Some of my favorite memories of time spent with my dad are related to pancakes. Those golden, mouth-watering, piping stacks of fluffy goodness smothered in maple syrup bring to mind countless moments at the kitchen table devouring his creations. Being asked "Would you like me to make you a pancake?" made you feel like you were the chosen child that day and were being treated to something quite special. Watching the process is an experience in and of itself. The cast iron skillet, the haphazard measurements, the lavish use of butter to grease the skillet and the pancake numerous times while it cooks, the sheer height of the flapjack, the blackened crispy outer layer, and the finesse with which he flips it. Not to mention the smoke that fills the kitchen at times. Then it is plated and ceremoniously drenched in our cousin Jack Laidlaw's maple syrup. Utter pancake perfection!

The ways in which Anne could write about this memory abound.
- Pancake recipe (expository)
- Instructions on how to make a pancake (expository)
- Descriptive paragraph (description)
- Recount of the experience (narrative)
- Personal memoir of the pancake event with Dad (narrative)
- Opinion piece about why pancakes are the best breakfast food ever (persuasive)
- Free verse poem about pancakes (descriptive)
- Food review (persuasive)

58   Third Step: Model the Habits of a Writer

We want to equip our writers with the ability to see ideas and topics through the lens of various forms and formats, just as Anne can with the pancake experience. This empowers an author to decide for themself which text type will best frame their writing. It allows writers to compose with greater confidence and ease, and express the message and purpose they want to convey with clarity.

The Block Party activity is designed to generate ideas according to the four frames of writing. Students are not required to write a sample; rather, they simply brainstorm ideas for a writing task. So gather some chart paper, markers, and small pieces of scrap paper to be ready to draft.

1. As a class, generate a list of nouns as potential writing topics; e.g., *running shoes, roses, chocolate bars, pine trees, yacht, monarch butterflies, blizzards, hockey, chocolate chip cookies, swimming*, etc.
2. Number students off 1 to 4 to create groups of four. Each group needs a captain and a materials person.
3. The materials person obtains a piece of chart paper, some markers, and four pieces of scrap paper. On each piece of scrap paper, the captain writes the letters D, E, P, or N. Then, the captain crumples the papers into a ball.
4. Each team member selects a ball of paper that indicates their assigned block on the chart.
5. The captain folds the chart paper in four or outlines four blocks. The captain writes the noun that has been chosen (either by the team or from the list of nouns brainstormed by the class) in the middle of the chart paper, and sets up the blocks in this way:

Block 1: D	Block 2: E
Block 3: P	Block 4: N

6. Block 1: Descriptive Writing
   On each ray of a sunshine web, a descriptive craft technique is used to describe the noun (e.g., simile/metaphor, onomatopoeia, strong verb, adjective, adverb, alliteration, etc.).
7. Block 2: Expository Writing
   Imagine a newspaper article about the noun and fill in the 5 W's and How. Write a headline that would grab the reader's interest across the top of the block.
8. Block 3: Persuasive Writing
   Draw a hand and write the noun in the palm. Write the following on the five fingertips: O for opinion; 1, 2, 3 for supporting arguments; C for the closing statement.
9. Block 4: Narrative Writing
   Write these headings on the outline of an open book, leaving space for answers: Title, Characters, Setting, Beginning/Intro, Middle/Problem, End/Solution. Think about a story that involves the noun and fill in the headings.
10. When the group is ready, students individually brainstorm ideas for their block.

This activity is adapted from Differentiated Instructional Strategies for Writing in the Content Areas, *by Carolyn Chapman and Rita King, 2003.*

11. At your signal, group members assist a teammate in generating ideas for their specific block, moving around the block clockwise.

Sample Block Party Brainstorms

Block 1: Descriptive Writing

                          Noun

Pancake: simile/metaphor: as fluffy as a pillow; adjectives/adverbs: a mouthful of golden cakey goodness; onomatopoeia: sizzle of the butter hitting the hot skillet; strong verb: the whomp of the pancake flapping onto the greased pan; alliteration: the perfectly plump pancake poised to enter your hungry mouth.

Block 2: Expository Writing

Pancake Tuesday
Who: Members of Lambeth Public School's Me to We Club
What: Pancake Day Sale with proceeds going to Clean Water Projects in Kenya
Where: Lambeth Public School Gymnasium
When: Tuesday, February 25
How: Members of the Me to We club measured, mixed and made pancakes by the hundreds on griddles in the school Activity Room. They served piping hot stacks of golden pancakes to all Primary and Junior students.
Headline: Local Students Raise Funds for Clean Water by Peddling Pancakes

Block 3: Persuasive Writing

Opinion: Pancakes are the perfect breakfast food for everyone.
1. A hot and filling food.
2. Quick and easy to make.
3. Sweet and tasty.
Closing: Wouldn't you love to have a hot and sweet treat like pancakes to start your day?

Block 4: Narrative Writing

Title: The Pancake Bandit
Characters: Dad, Anne, Roy the Dog
Setting: Anne's dad's kitchen
Beginning/Intro: On a snowy Sunday morning, Anne's dad is whipping up his world-famous pancakes.
Middle/Problem: As each perfect pancake hits the plate and is covered in maple syrup, it quickly disappears. No one knows who is stealing the precious flapjacks.
End/Solution: A trail of sticky footprints lead to the dog bed in the living room where Roy, the precocious Black Lab dog, is licking the last traces of syrup from his chops.

The Habit of Planning *When*

As important as knowing what we're going to write is deciding when we're going to do it. As teachers, we traditionally expect students to read nightly; however, how often do we ask students to write at home? Have you ever asked students to gather ideas in preparation for writing the next day as an at-home activity? Do we allow students to travel between home and school with their notebooks? Have you encouraged students to continue their drafts at home? Do we invite students to write freely and frequently on their own time? How often do we give students the time and opportunity to share their compositions, honoring their initiative and commitment?

We're not talking about students creating perfectly polished pieces of text. Rather, we need to be invested in developing their writing life inside and outside of school. For many students, writing is something they do exclusively at school for teachers, not for themselves or purely for enjoyment. Writing probably isn't even on student's radar for their weekly to-do list. We believe it is essential that we are frank and forthright with our students: becoming a writer requires a time commitment and dedication on their part.

Literacy leader Donald Graves launched a movement back in 1985 that changed the way we taught writing. In his article "All Children Can Write" he spoke eloquently about children's innate desire to write, what writing is, the process, and how to teach writing. In particular he addressed the paramount issue of time:

> Our data show that children need to write a minimum of 4 days a week to see any appreciable change in the quality of their writing. It takes that amount of writing to contribute to their personal development as learners. Unless children write at least 4 days a week, they won't like it. Once-a-week writing (the national average is about 1 day in 8) merely reminds them they can't write; they never write often enough to listen to their writing… When children write on a daily basis, we find they write when they aren't writing. Children get into their subjects, thinking about their texts and topics when they are riding on buses, lying in bed, watching television, reading books, or taking trips. When they write regularly, papers accumulate. There is visible evidence they know and are growing. They gain experience in choosing topics and very soon have more topics to write about than class time can accommodate. (Graves, 1985)

We can add to Graves' findings the work of Lamott, Routman, Calkins, Newkirk, Fletcher, Gallagher, Kittle, Romano, Reif, and Heard—the list of literacy leaders who believe in the importance of daily writing time is long. Please add our names to that list. The case is strong and closed—kids have to write often, because time spent writing begets writing will.

Let's Make a Deal

Have you ever been in a position where you have had to negotiate or barter the price you pay for a product? Some people relish the opportunity; for the rest of us it is anxiety-inducing. We want to settle on a price that is a fair and equitable. Neither seller nor buyer wants to be taken advantage of. Luckily, in the writing opportunities we sell to our students, everybody walks away a winner—no stress involved. As the lead writer in the room, building relationships with your students as writers, the first deal you make is committing to giving them time each and every day to exercise themselves as writers. Your students, in turn, are expected to carve out time to develop the habit of writing outside of school. To

---

Students will
- begin to develop the habit of a daily writer, inside and outside the classroom
- recognize that developing this habit requires a time commitment, dedication, and intentionality on their part

help them navigate their schedules, show students how to catch and capture incidental time throughout the day for drafting. Here's the deal:
- You commit to giving students time each and every day to exercise themselves as writers
- Your students commit to carving out time to develop the habits of a writer at home
- Together, you catch and capture undedicated minutes for writing time.

The Commitment of Time

Let's show students how invested we are in their development as writers by providing them with writing time every day. This is an essential habit for your class to become a writing community, and for individual students to develop stamina as writers. It is vital time and a fixture in the schedule. A Bus Safety presentation, a field trip to Apple Land, or concert rehearsals cannot get in the way of providing students with an opportunity to practice their writing. At the beginning of the school year, be explicit and direct with your students that every day you are going to give them a wonderful gift—the gift of time. Time to explore their thoughts and ideas for writing. Time to get wrapped up in character development and story creation. Time to investigate their own wonders and find the answers to their burning questions. Time to experience the social and emotional rewards of being a writer.

Students need to understand how precious this time is and that they are expected to use this opportunity to develop as a writer. As teachers, we view this time as two-fold: teach and practice. It is essential that we explicitly teach our students idea development, the various forms and formats, craft techniques, and how to use mentors in their own writing, all during scheduled writing time; subsequently, we guarantee that students have time to practice, apply, and play independently. However, the time given to teach and practice cannot be simplified into definite allotments of minutes. It fluctuates, depending on student need, the writing project, and where writers are at in the writing process. We must be flexible but accountable to honoring our commitment.

> The beginning of the year will look different from the end of the year as your students build writing stamina. So be realistic in terms of how long your students can sustain independent writing at the outset of the year, especially since some students will not have engaged in this worthy activity over the summer holidays. As well, the time you allot to writing will vary depending on the grade and age of students you teach.

Carving Out Time to Be a Writer Outside of School

As we develop the habit of daily writing in class, it is essential that we expect students to develop a writing life beyond the walls of the classroom. At school we create the ideal conditions for students to engage in this valuable practice: we provide the time, space, materials, and sometimes ideas with which to write. But if the writing habit is school- and teacher-dependent, how do students own the habit? They can only do that with the added expectation that they nurture the habits of a writer on their own time. Daily writing in class benefits students; however, this is often not enough time to develop the habits of a writer for most students. When we acknowledge that a fair amount of class writing time is driven by curriculum demands, it is essential that students develop the routine of carving out the time and space in their at-home lives for free writing. Only doing that will they become writers for life.

Students have a variety of activities they are committed to and engage in outside of school. We encourage you to examine completed student Writing Surveys (see page 47) and pay close attention to the responses to question 1: *If you had a chance to write every day would you: yes or no?* and question 4: *Do you choose to write in your spare time; yes or no?* Tally student responses and share the results with the class. Facilitate a discussion about some of the obstacles to developing a writing habit outside of school. What do you notice? What are the things that get in the way of your students' writing? Consider having learners respond in writing to following prompt: *I would have more time to write for pleasure if...* Are there commonalities among your students' responses? Which students are highly scheduled and therefore have less flexibility? Which ones are proficient time wasters? Which ones have trouble finding ideas? Which ones have difficulty finding a space that is conducive for writing? And which ones just don't enjoy writing yet?

Catching and Capturing

Knowing that students lead very busy lives opens the door to discussing the opportunity to catch and capture time—time that is not spent engaged in a specific activity; bits and pieces of time that float around our days unaccounted for. Share various time scenarios with students that are relevant to their daily lives. For example:

> *This weekend you are going to a tournament that is two-and-a-half hours away. Have you considered taking your Thought Jot book along to record the countless ideas that come to mind on the journey?*

> *Your family is going for your annual dental cleaning. While your sister is getting her pearly whites checked, what are you doing? Watching the screens or reading outdated magazines? No! You are getting lost drafting in your Writer's Notebook.*

> *"I'm done!" How many times a day do you say or think that? Well, no need to ask me what you can do now, because these snippets of time can always be spent developing ideas in our Writer's Notebooks!*

Stealing time to jot, draft, and experiment is key to growing and developing as a writer. Consider at the end of each week having students brainstorm or share times and places they captured and caught extra writing time. This can provide the entire class with ideas for when they can steal some extra time themselves.

The Habit of Planning *Where*

So students know what they are going to write. They know when they are going to do it. But do they know where they will write outside of school? What specific places enable them to escape from it all and dive into imagining, generating, jotting, playing, and composing without being distracted? Passionate writers can readily name their writing haunts.

A Huffington Post article "Where Do Writers Write" (2017) shared the environments three authors wrote in. The interviewer asked published authors to reveal their favorite locations: messy desk, library, subway train, café. Each author had a distinct place that fit them, a tried and true location to compose. Our young writers must also discover locations that enable their writing to flourish. A desk in their bedroom, at the kitchen table, a cozy chair in the living room, a window seat in the den overlooking the backyard. Just like published authors, our students need to seek out places that let their ideas flow.

> *Anne*
>
> My writing locations appear to be driven by the type of writing I am doing. When engaged in work-driven writing, my writing space seems to always be the dining room table beside a massive picture window that looks out onto the pond and open farm fields. When I am playing in my Writer's Notebook, I can usually be found on the chaise longue beside the fireplace in my back kitchen, where I frequently gaze out the window. These places enable me to be alone with my own thoughts and provide space to reflect and muse quietly.

Where is your writing space at home: a desk in your home office by the window, a comfortable chair in the den, propped up in your bed? Each of us has our favorite spot to write. For many, these locations have certain things in common. They are often quiet, relaxed, and calm. The physical spaces enable our mental space to be free from the distractions, demands, and disruptions that crowd our mind and can get in the way of our creativity. As students grow as writers they begin to establish writing nooks around their homes, places where they can relax and immerse themselves in writing. We must support our developing writers as they uncover places where they can engage in writing, free from interruptions and distractions.

All the Places We Love to Write

Students will
- *share and discover the places they enjoy writing*

A great way to launch a conversation about the places students enjoy writing is to read aloud our adaption of the poem "Quiet Morning" by Karen Winnick.

Quiet Writing Morning
It's early in the morning
Writer's Notebook, pen and me
Sitting at the kitchen table
Just we three.
Gazing out the window
Thoughts flow free
Life's little moments
Writer's Notebook, pen and me.

After reading the poem, encourage your students to share all the places they enjoy writing outside of school. Explore the characteristics of each place: quiet, solitary, comfy, nature-infused (window), bustling, etc. Record student thinking on a chart.

The Habit of Acting: Thinking

As we set out to create a writing community, it is essential that we assess and evaluate our students' preconceived thoughts and ideas about writing and clear up any misconceptions. What is their working definition of what writing is? Do they describe a writer as someone who can spell all the words accurately, can write legibly, and knows all the punctuation and grammar rules? Yes, these are some of characteristics of quality writing, but do students realize that there is much more that makes writing powerful and appealing to the ear and engaging to the reader? You need to ask the question: *What is writing?*

Writing Is…

> Students will
> - share and grow their definition of writing

Initially, many developing writers have a very narrow definition of what writing is. They pay attention to the overt actions, the aspects of writing that can be seen on the page. But they are less aware of the covert actions, what happens inside the writer's head and heart while composing text that is unseen. Our writers must become acquainted and very familiar with the thinking that goes hand-in-hand with writing, the invisible actions that take place in their brain that contribute to the writing process.

1. Prepare sheets with a sentence stem written on each:

   Writing is…

   Writing takes…

   Writing means…

   Writing involves…

   Writing includes…

   Color code papers according to sentence stem so students can easily distinguish between them.

2. Distribute one sheet to each student. Students are expected to respond to their sentence stem anonymously. Be sure to let students know that they will be trading pages multiple times so be sure to leave space for others to write.

3. Mix and mingle five times, until each student has responded to each sentence stem once. Once students have documented their thinking about writing, gather them together.

4. Select one sentence stem and share the variety of responses students have made. Allow students time to consider the similarities and differences between responses.

5. Repeat step 3 for each sentence stem over the next few days, depending on student engagement and time.

6. After exploring the variety of responses, summarize and consolidate the thinking of the class:

   > *If we want to summarize all of the responses we shared over the last few days, I wonder what we would say. Is there a common idea that represents what writing is? We might come up with this: Writing is an expression that involves time, effort, energy, and thought.*

> Students will
> - witness the variety of thoughts, ideas, decisions, and moves writers make when constructing a piece of text
>
> We recommend dedicating a series of lessons at the outset of the year to writing out loud.

Writing Out Loud

In *Strategies that Work*, Harvey and Goudvis detail the thinking routine they call "leaving tracks of thinking and inner conversation"; Chris Tovani calls this strategy "annotating the text." Whatever you choose to call it, the process involves paying attention to the thinking taking place during reading to make meaning. Let's apply the same principal to the writing process to shed light on the thinking and decisions that writers make when crafting text.

> *Anne and Mary*
>
> Our friend Stephanie Cook is a gifted writer. She communicates eloquently, whether it is a story, explanation, or thank-you letter. In her classroom, she skilfully thinks out loud, sharing the countless decisions and moves she makes as she crafts text. Her students hang on her every word and on every mark of her pen as she composes. Sometimes it appears effortless, while at other times she stumbles and fumbles to narrow an idea, to say things clearly, to find the right word, or to spell something accurately. When she thinks aloud, her students have front-row seats to a writer in action. As the community grows and develops in their ability and understanding, Stephanie intentionally invites her students into the writing process. She elicits the ideas and thoughts of students and weaves their thinking into her pieces. This illustrates clearly to students that she values their input and contributions; above all, it communicates to them that she sees them as cowriters to be relied on.

Writing out loud for some of us is a nerve-wracking and risky exercise. A piece of chart paper, a marker, and 25 eager faces can indeed be intimidating, especially when the writing does not flow readily and we struggle and strain to compose a piece of text. But we believe that our students need to see this; they must watch the challenge and witness the effort a writer puts forth to create a meaningful passage. We admit that too often we have misled our writers by having a text pre-written or perfectly planned out prior to live writing, and have merely rewritten or replicated it in front of our students. This leaves developing writers with a false impression of what writing involves, what it takes. When they inevitably struggle themselves, they believe that they cannot write and are not a writer. So, writing out loud is vitally important and must include a level of authenticity. We want our writers to understand that we think deeply, specifically, and intentionally while we draft text, and that this inner conversation facilitates and cultivates rich writing.

1. Introduce the concept:

   Each and every time you pick up a pen to draft, you and the pen are having a conversation. An inner discussion is taking place inside your head. Have you ever considered that you are talking with the pen the entire time you are writing? I see that some of you are shaking your heads.

   Today we are going to try to listen to what our writing brain is deciding and determining. While I'm writing, I am going to open up my writing brain and tell you what I'm thinking inside my head. You will hear and see how my inner conversation translates to words on the page. So let's start…

2. While writing aloud in front of students, stop at strategic points to model your inner conversation. Demonstrate the variety of thinking taking place in your writing brain as you attempt to compose a piece of text in front of them.

- Select topic and format: descriptive paragraph about the best part of me (in the style of "The Best Part of Me" by Wendy Ewald)
- Narrow the topic: determine which physical attribute best represents me
- Pre-writing: what in particular you want to share and explore in your paragraph

3. Record your thinking on an anchor chart.
4. After thinking aloud and drafting a few more lines, encourage students to turn-and-talk to share with a peer their thoughts about what they see and hear you doing as a writer. Students might identify that you thoughtfully modeled aloud various lead sentences before committing one to paper; carefully drafted sentences that bring your physical attribute to life in the reader's mind using descriptive details; used sensory language and a variety of craft techniques; intentionally used a thesaurus for word variety, etc.
5. Continue the write-aloud, stopping at intervals so students can turn, talk, and share what they see and hear. Record their thoughts on the chart.
6. After writing, review the ideas generated and listed on the chart. Begin to label student thinking into larger categories; i.e., Ideas, Organization, Sentence Fluency, Word Choice, Voice, Descriptive Devices, Craft Techniques, Format Features, etc.

Since writing-aloud slows down the writing process considerably, the text will not be finished in one sitting. This models for students that writing doesn't go from start to finish in one session.

Students will
- explore the various writing traits and features that writers use to compose text

The Writing Brain

Since your writers are now aware of the inner conversation that occurs as they compose text, and the many complex decisions and moves a writer makes, it is time to label the traits and features that contribute to expressing their thoughts, ideas, and feelings in writing. The Writing Brain graphic on page 83 is a tangible way to make the covert workings of the brain visible. Display it in a place of prominence so that it can be referred to frequently and provide an anchor for writing conversations.

1. Refer to the anchor chart created during Writing Out Loud lessons to review the various features and traits writers use to express themselves meaningfully and effectively.
2. Label the traits and features and celebrate the array of intentional writing moves authors make.
3. Introduce the Writing Brain graphic to identify or review the writing traits and features writers use.
4. Select a few students who are willing to share with the class a piece of text they have written in their Writer's Notebook. Interview the author and determine the intentional moves and decisions they made in their writing. Track the traits and features each writer used on the Writing Brain to notice and celebrate their thinking.

Extension

Following independent writing time, have students track the thinking/traits/features they used in crafting a piece of text by coloring in parts of the My Writing Brain template on page 84. As they color in particular sections over several days, students will begin to note which traits and features they use frequently and which they rarely use, as well as to contemplate the relationship between the type of text they are writing and the traits and features they utilize.

The Habit of Acting: Thinking 67

The Habit of Acting: Reading

Each of us can remember a time when we were captivated by a story that was read aloud to us. We have been stopped in our tracks and have reread a line so that we can savor it again. The intentional choice of words is like candy to our ears, creates vivid images in our minds, and elicits emotions that move us. The written text and the manner in which it is read aloud creates a synergy that strikes at the head and heart of the reader. The author has left the reader intentional cues and clues on how to read the text. The way in which the piece is organized, the word choice, the phrasing of sentences, and skilfully woven craft techniques create a beautiful tapestry of text. Drawing students' attention to these traits during read-alouds provides a starting point for future writing conversations. By reading a text together, the whole class shares a common experience that anchors our writing conversations and can provide inspiration for our developing writers.

Read-Alouds to Illuminate the Power of Writing

Students will
- be immersed in quality text
- understand the value and power of writing to impact readers
- become aware that writing will document a moment in time that can be relived again and again
- understand the connection between reading and writing, and learn to listen as a writer to gather craft

They say that imitation is the highest form of flattery—and this applies to writing. We want students to emulate phenomenal writers. Since we can't physically bring a writer into the classroom each day, we do the next best thing by bringing authors' art into the room in the form of their books during read aloud. We intentionally select, read, and draw students' attention to the exemplary craft found in text so they can use them as mentors in their own writing. So let's ensure that our students are reading text that is chock full of writing potential. According to Dorfman and Cappelli, "A mentor text is a book that offers myriad possibilities for our students and for ourselves as writers" (Dorfman and Cappelli, 2007, p. 3). Mentor texts can stimulate ideas, introduce new writing formats, offer unique text structures, model craft techniques, present distinctive word choice, and ignite a passion for writers to mine their own lives for writing possibilities. Our reaction to writing mentors shows our students the value we place on the author's words to touch and move our hearts, minds, and hands. Don't let the words rush over you quickly like a waterfall; instead, slow down your reading and relish the moment.

When our purpose for a read-aloud is to influence and inspire our young writers, we need to intentionally select texts that fit the bill. As the lead reader/writer in the classroom, we must draw students' attention to writer's craft techniques found in quality text; however, not during the first read—that is for pure enjoyment. Most young readers and writers don't notice the craft techniques authors use to communicate vividly to their readers, and there was a time when we didn't either. It's not a lack of ability to identify these techniques, rather a lack of experience in doing so. It is our job to slow down the reading to share our excitement and enthusiasm for beautiful writing. We must revisit powerful parts that demand a second read. As well, we must name and label specific craft techniques that writers use. That way we enable students to recognize these techniques in their independent reading; once this happens, they are empowered to read with a writer's eye. In our experience, once students are aware of specific craft techniques of alliteration, simile, magic of three, proper nouns/brand names, etc., there is no stopping them.

> ### *Picture Books for all Ages*
>
> The quality texts we expose our students to and immerse them in at the beginning of the year are predominately picture books. This sometimes comes as a surprise to Junior and Intermediate students, many of whom think that picture books are no longer age-appropriate for them and hold no value. They couldn't be more wrong! These books are the perfect stimulus for writing:
> - Their length allows teachers to peruse an assortment to find the best fit for readers/writers and purpose.
> - Their length means that they don't take a tremendous time commitment to explore.
> - They pack a punch in few pages and serve as a model for the kind of writing we may ask students to craft.
> - The illustrations appeal to the aesthetic in each of us.

We select texts to be read aloud during writing lessons for a variety of purposes:
- for exposure to different kinds of writing
- to experience a range of emotions
- as a mentor text for writing
- as a stimulus for idea generation

We have chosen books that focus on the value of writing, that demonstrate the emotional impact writing has on readers, that show the ability of writing to stimulate ideas, to familiarize students with formats, and as mentor texts for writing.

Not just any book is going to accomplish these things or have this effect. We believe that exposing our students to and immersing our students in quality text is fundamental. The text needs to be intellectually demanding, promote sustained classroom conversations, and be rich enough to serve as a model for either format, traits, or craft. Mindfully select different themes you want to tackle through books.

Writers Write

In our early days with a class, we want to target books that honor and celebrate writing. Hearing about the writing adventures of others, their experiences and escapades, students begin see the value writing holds. Recommended books include the following:

Mary Jane and Herm Auch, *The Plot Chickens*
Kate Banks, *Max's Words*
Barbara Bottner, *Miss Brooks' Story Nook*
Eileen Christelow, *What Do Authors Do?*
Brianne Farley, *Ike's Incredible Ink*
Abby Hanlon, *Ralph Tells a Story*
Joan Holub, *Little Red Writing*
Helen Lester, *Author: A True Story*
Susan Allen and Jane Lindaman, *Written Anything Good Lately?*
Eileen Spinelli, *The Best Story*
Roni Schotter, *Nothing Ever Happens on 90th Street*

Edited by Elissa Brent Weissman, *Our Story Begins – Your Favorite Authors and Illustrators Share Fun, Inspiring, and Occasionally Ridiculous Things They Wrote and Drew as Kids*

Heart Books

Have you ever stained the pages of a book with your tears? Shouted aloud at the characters? Or even tossed a text aside in anguish? The written word has undeniable power. Young writers need to know that writing has the ability to move, inspire, touch, aggravate, change, persuade, anger, and motivate its readers. Take them on this emotional roller coaster through read-alouds, so that students experience the range of emotions the written word draws out of readers. Recommended books include the following:

Eve Bunting, *Gleam and Glow*
Jenny Kay Dupuis, *I Am Not a Number*
Lucy Falcone, *I Didn't Stand Up*
Peter Golenbock, *Teammates*
Ellen Levine, *Henry's Freedom Box*
Trudy Ludwig, *The Invisible Boy*
Rosemary McCarney, *The Way to School*
Judith Viorst, *The Tenth Good Thing About Barney*
Rebecca Upjohn, *Lily and the Paper Man*
Eric Walters, *My Name is Blessing*
Margaret Wild, *The Very Best of Friends*
Jacqueline Woodson, *Each Kindness*

It's Time to Laugh

According to author and renowned speaker Chuck Gallozzi, "Laughter dissolves tension, stress, anxiety, irritation, anger, grief, and depression… after a hearty bout of laughter, you will experience a sense of well-being. Simply put, he who laughs, lasts" (Gallozzi, 2009). We believe it is important to mindfully inject fun and humor into our early read-alouds. These books signal to students that one of the reasons people write is to entertain their readers. They need to know that not all texts explore serious topics and that there is a lighter side to writing. Laughter is infectious, brings us together, and fills our classrooms with joy. And who doesn't want to share in the laughter? Recommended books include the following:

Babette Cole, *The Sprog Owner's Manual*
Kelly DiPucchio, *Zombie in Love*
Elise Gravel, Disgusting Critters Series: *The Fly; The Worm; The Rat; The Slug; Head Lice; The Toad*
Trinka Hakes Noble, *Meanwhile Back at the Ranch*
Bob Hartman, *The Wolf Who Cried Boy*
Lester Laminack, *Three Hens and a Peacock*
Steven Layne, *My Brother Dan's Delicious*
Robert Munsch, *I Have to Go; Thomas' Snowsuit; Show and Tell; Mud Puddle; Alligator Baby*
Jenny Offill, *11 Experiments That Failed*
Edited by Jon Scieszka, *Guys Reading - Funny Business*

Janet Stevens, *Help Me, Mr. Mutt!: Expert Answer for Dogs with People Problems*
Mark Teague, *Dear Mrs. LaRue*

Books that Stimulate Writing

How many times has a text stirred up your own memories or adventures? Perhaps it was the problem, a character, the conflict, or the setting that reminded you of someone or something. And before you know it you are recalling your own experiences. Such texts often serve as idea-generators for writers. We cannot always know what within the pages of book will spark a memory for students, but there are texts that deal with universal topics and themes that the majority of us can relate and connect to. For example, the Franklin books by Paulette Bourgeois make up a series that addresses a lot of typical life events for young children: telling a lie, making new friends, learning to ride a bike, getting lost, being afraid of the dark, birthdays, holidays, etc. By intentionally selecting texts with universal topics and themes, we can stimulate the writer in all of us. Try books about

- Celebrations
- Feelings
- Conflicts
- Friendships
- Death
- Family Dynamics
- Bullying
- Adventures: e.g., road trips, holidays, camp
- Human Rights
- Our Natural World

Flavorful Formats

> *Mary*
>
> Recently I went with my husband Peter to Broderick's Ice Cream Parlour in Port Stanley with friends for a summer treat. The menu there includes around fifty flavors: moosetracks, Naniamo bar, Niagara peach, rum raisin, St. Jacobs apple pie, to name a few. Since I am a frequent visitor and have sampled many of the flavors, the decision of what to get in my homemade waffle cone is less daunting than for those first-time customers who are overwhelmed by the list of unique tastes.

Like first-time visitors to Broderick's, writers are often unfamiliar with the menu. They lack an awareness of all the forms and formats their writing can take, so they rely on the same ones over and over again. As a result, the quality and impact of their writing can be compromised because the format they have chosen does not best fit their purpose and/or audience. While the wealth of rewards and value that can be found in narrative picture books is immense, we need our read-alouds to draw from a variety of formats and genre. We must be mindful to frequently draw students' attention to form and format throughout the day and across subject areas. Be sure to include stories, poems, articles,

Students will
- understand the connection between reading and writing and learn to listen as a writer to gather craft

reports, comics, jokes, letters, and infographics. Our writers need to be exposed to all the different flavors their writing can take.

Replicating our Favorite Writers

We must revisit powerful texts that demand a second read. We must draw students' attention to specific sections, lines, phrases, and words that are music to our ears. As well, we must name and label specific craft techniques that writers use. In this way, we enable students to recognize these techniques in their independent reading; once this happens, they are empowered to read with a writer's eye. Once students are aware of specific craft techniques of alliteration, simile, magic of three, proper nouns/brand names, etc., the quality of their own writing is elevated.

Samples below are from a book that stands out for both of us in terms of stunning language, expertly used craft techniques, and captivating message: *Leah's Pony* by Elizabeth Friedrich.

Samples of The Magic of Three

The hot, dry, dusty days kept coming.
All week Leah worried and waited and wondered what to do.

Sample of Repetition

It was hard for Leah to keep her pony's coat shining. It was hard for Mama to keep the house clean. It was hard for Papa to carry buckets of water for the sow and her piglets.

Papa's best bull. Sold. Mama's prize rooster. Sold. Leah's favourite calf. Sold.

Sample of Simile

Leah scratched that special spot under her pony's mane and brushed him till his coat glistened like satin.

Samples of Alliteration

The pony was strong and swift and sturdy, with just a snip of white at the end of his soft black nose.

That whole summer, Leah and her pony crossed cloud-capped corn fields, and chased cattle through the pasture.

Sample of Using Proper Nouns/Brand Names

Farmall Tractor

We encourage you to keep an anchor chart of all these techniques.

Samples of Vivid Verbs

She raced her pony past empty fields lined with dry gullies. She galloped past a house with rags stuffed in broken windowpanes. She sped right past Mr. B. sweeping the steps outside his store.

Sometimes on those hot, dry nights, Leah heard Papa and Mama's hushed voices whispering in the kitchen.

The Habit of Acting: Talking

Have you ever heard the phrase "a well-oiled machine" used to describe something that operates and functions smoothly through coordinated movements? Bicycles, chainsaws, hinges, the Tin Man from the Wizard of Oz—items that benefit from frequent oiling are many. This type of maintenance enables parts to move effortlessly and efficiently. Our writers also benefit from being "oiled" routinely so their writing flows. An essential component of a writing community is talk: talking to generate ideas; talking with peers to compose stories; talking about mentors; talking about the power of craft techniques to enhance writing; talking to improve the quality and clarity of our writing. Talk is a foundational block of a vibrant writing community.

Oral Storytelling

The benefits of oral story making are endless. In *Making Stories* Irene Watts extols the value of this activity. She states, "The creation of… stories encourages language, imagination, spontaneity, confidence, a grasp of plot, a sense of tension and drama… [it] explores the universe" (Watts, 1992, pg. 10). In the book *Children as Storytellers*, Kerry Mallan concurs that orally telling stories fosters imagination, creativity, the exploration of new possibilities; increases active participation; develops skills in story schema, listening comprehension skills, understanding of self and others, and higher-level thinking skills; and overall plays a critical role in the development of reading and writing (Mallan, 1991, pg. 9–15). So let's empower our students to find their voices and use their imaginations to compose on-the-fly tales that are silly, serious, funny, scary, heart-wrenching, outlandish, heart-warming, and fun! The playfulness, freedom, and risk-taking of storytelling provides an injection of self-confidence for our writers.

Picture Prompt Story

Display a thought-provoking image to the class on a chart or the interactive whiteboard. For example, an image of gum stuck to a running shoe, a child opening an enormous present, a picture of a group of students running toward a finish line, etc. Share with students that the image represents the beginning/middle/ or end of the story. Have students turn and talk with a partner to orally create a short story about the event. Students will be eager to share their unique and original story with classmates. Be sure to draw students' attention to the fact that an image can spark multiple and varied ideas, that stories follow a traditional structure (i.e., problem/solution and beginning/middle/end), and that events should be logically sequenced.

Student Sample: Ashley's Picture Prompt Writing

Build a Story

To write a collaborative story, bring the class together and sit in a circle. Choose an engaging story starter to spark everyone's imaginations:

- I couldn't believe my eyes…
- Suddenly the lights went out…
- At the community yard sale, I found an old set of keys. Little did I know things would never be the same…

Many times we wished we had recorded the oral compositions so that a permanent record remained to be read and enjoyed again and again. Not surprisingly, often versions of stories using the same sentence starter would crop up in Writer's Notebooks.

- *Bang! Bang! Bang!* went the knock on the door…
- Who knew that one decision would change Tom's life…

The story is created around the circle as each student adds a sentence that builds on the one that preceded it. This requires intentional listening in order for students to be able to creatively and logically move the story forward.

More Than One Story

1. With the class, generate a list of options for each of the following categories: Character, Setting, Problem. Record each idea on a separate color-coded recipe card (one color for each category).
2. Randomly draw a card from each set. Using the selections, collaboratively create an oral story.
3. Each time a set of cards is drawn from the piles, a new story is born.
4. Afterward, students may choose this as a strategy to explore on their own for generating a composition in their writer's notebook.

> We have found that when students generate ideas as a class, the ideas are applicable and relevant to their interest and age.

The Habit of Acting: Sharing

Writers share their writing. They gravitate toward each other. They long to talk about the characters they have created, the enchanted settings they have brought to life, and the stories they have crafted. They are eager to share their developing ideas and explore how to best bring them to life on the page. When they experience struggles and face uncertainty, they benefit from having a fellow writer listen to their writing and offer suggestions, advice, and feedback. A writing community is an integral part of a writing life. The reasons we share are endless:

- It creates bonds among writers.
- It inspires developing writers to look at their own writing with a critical lens.
- It motivates writers to aspire to greater proficiency and quality in their writing.
- It celebrates growth, risk-taking, and accomplishment.
- It honors the play and struggle that is inherent in writing.
- It deepens students' investment and respect for the creative process.
- It broadens perspective by exposing students to different writing styles and techniques.
- It enables learning to accept feedback from others and apply it to work.
- It affects and enhances the quality of writing.
- It allows us to push and move students to deeper thinking.
- It provides us with the opportunity to assess student writing on the fly.

Students traditionally are asked and expected to share their drafts at writing conferences and for assessment purposes. Teachers are the primary audience, as we provide feedback, guidance, acknowledgment, and a grade for student work. Although this type of sharing has its time and place, it can be exceptionally narrow and limiting. We must create opportunities and structures in our classrooms that enable writers to authentically share their writing in purposeful ways. Sharing with a trusted writing partner, classmate, learning buddy, family, school community, and beyond expands the definition of audience in a palpable manner. Writers come to understand that their writing has the capacity to entertain others, to educate and inform readers, to forge connections, and to be a source of inspiration—all by sharing. As Mary always says, "When students feel heard, they write." But don't just take our word for why sharing is important. Listen to what some of our students have exclaimed about the power of sharing:

- "It lets me show the world what I think—my creativity and my mind."
- "I like to listen to others and hear their ideas and imagination. And if I like it I ask to borrow their idea."
- "I like to share on the sharing chair. People get to know what your story is. You don't hold it in. When you hold it in, it is like nobody cares."
- "I like to share my ideas and get a response, to find out what they think."
- "I like to listen because I get to compare my ideas to what they wrote and see differences. I think inside my head 'I like that—I'm going to do that next time.'"
- "Friends help me make my writing better."
- "I get to show my class the kind of writing I can do and inspire them."

You can imagine the power and pride students experience when a response to their writing comes to them from within or beyond the classroom. This speaks to the highly social nature of writing. Here are some ways to promote writers:

- Place students' published work in a place of honor within the classroom.
- Display work on bulletin boards in the class or hallway for others to enjoy.
- Feature published pieces in the school monthly newsletter or website.
- Frame student writing and strategically display around the school.
- Publish student writing in your classroom newsletter each month. Ensure that all members of the class have been featured by the end of the year.
- Display student writing in businesses around the neighborhood for the community to enjoy.
- Invite students to trade pieces of writing with a classmate to take home and share. Provide a comment sheet so the author can receive encouraging feedback/comments from others.
- Have author parties in your classroom to feature student work. Invite visitors to join in the fun!
- Create cross-grade partnerships so students can teach each other writing techniques they have learned.

Private vs Public Writing

In *Bird by Bird: Some Instructions on Writing and Life*, Anne Lamott eloquently states, "Writing…is about some of our deepest needs: our need to be visible, to be heard, our need to make sense of our lives, to wake up and grow and belong" (1995, p. 19). While sharing our writing with a wider audience has tremendous merit and value, there are times when the content of our writing is too private, precious, and personal for others to view and consume. The writing was for the author's eyes only and, while the act of writing these intimate thoughts is cathartic, it also makes the author vulnerable. You, too, might have written something that was only for you, or perhaps you have written something to another person but never intended for them to see it. The writing alone was enough. This writing is not about getting feedback, improving craft, receiving accolades, or inspiring others. It comes from a place of personal release of

> emotion, contributing to our emotional wellness. Examples of things students' private writing might be about include the loss of a pet, a parent not showing up for their scheduled visit, a personal failure or embarrassment, a community tragedy that affects them. Typically this writing comes from free writing opportunities and resides in our students' Writer's Notebooks. In these cases, direct young writers to merely fold the page over to ensure privacy and to signal that the writing is for their eyes only. Providing our students with opportunities to share their writing publicly while honoring the fact that some of their writing commands privacy recognizes both the social and singular nature of writing.

Formal Sharing Techniques

Author's Chair

Cara Rae Clements' Sharing Stump

Classroom chair, stool, rocking chair, stump, or cozy armchair—you need to have a special perch for authors to read from. It becomes a place of honor that students are eager and proud to occupy. Just as a talking stick in many classrooms garners respect and holds attentiveness of classmates, this sacred seat honors the work and voice of the author and commands the attention and respect of classmates. The purpose of sitting in the author's chair depends on student need: to celebrate a published piece, to problem-solve a tricky spot, to get feedback on an idea, to motivate others with use of craft, to entertain, to break through writer's block, etc.

Hot Off the Press

Celebrating the writers in your room by spotlighting their work will support the vibrancy of your writing community. Consider designating a special shelf, bin, or binder to feature student writing in the classroom. For example, if students have recently completed a writing report on endangered species, be sure to print a class set of their investigations and encourage students to read them during independent reading time. Expanding the audience beyond the teacher recognizes the time and effort that goes into taking a piece of text through the entire writing process.

Sometimes quick writes, on-demand pieces, and Writer's Notebook entries deserve to be highlighted within the classroom, too. We have found that requesting permission from a student to publicly share their writing on an easel/stand in the room sends the message that we believe their writing has merit, that it holds value, and that each stage of the writing process is significant. So take time each week to flag entries in Writer's Notebooks that could be featured. Consider laminating or placing photocopied excerpts in page protectors on stands for all to see. You may want to add a Notable Note directing the reader to notice a particular feature in the text: catchy lead sentence, masterful craft technique, dazzling description, skilful character development, etc. You'll be pleasantly surprised by the number of students who wander over to browse the latest selections!

Lines that Linger

It's that line that makes you pause. It begs to be reread. You cannot help but slow down and savor it. It lingers and lasts in the reader's brain. Lines like this need to lifted from the page and documented for the entire class to see, hear, and appreciate. Record these lines of love on an anchor chart, acknowledging the source and author. Sometimes the snippets are taken from commercially published texts; just as frequently they are taken from our own students' pieces. A public chart serves to recognize an author's expertise as well as providing a mentor text for others.

Informal Sharing Techniques

Put Down the Pen

As we write this book, we are constantly taking our fingers off the keys and rereading what we have drafted. We listen to the words as they roll off our tongues to ensure they communicate the message clearly, effectively, and as eloquently as possible. Writers frequently stop and reread their work, but this is not automatic for our developing writers, who are much more inclined to write from start to finish without stopping to reflect. By asking students to put down their pens and read over what they have drafted, you can instill in them this essential habit. Once pens are down, request that students embark on reading with attention to expression and intonation to get a keen sense of what the text will sound like to the reader/audience. Ask them to note any rough patches, unclear segments, or spots that might require an injection of detail, word choice, and/or craft. As well, invite students to share a lead sentence, a favorite line, a detailed paragraph, or a quick write draft with a peer or the entire class. This informal sharing builds your writing community by igniting excitement and injecting energy in the midst of writing.

Trading Texts

Teacher feedback is necessary for our writers to develop and grow in their ability to craft quality text. Feedback needs to be timely, specific, and relevant; however, this time-consuming task often cannot be provided for every piece a student drafts nor at the most opportune time. So ask peers to become feedback providers in your writing community. When we trade texts and model for students how to provide feedback, we share in the work of elevating the artistry of every writer in the room. A structure we use to guide student responses to writing is offering Warm Thoughts/Cool Comments: Warm Thoughts are the compliments, praise, and shout-outs for things the reader wants to applaud and celebrate in the writing they have been given; Cool Comments can be questions, suggestions, advice, or ideas for improvement the reader would like the writer to consider to uplift their work.

Craft Conversations

Everything takes practice. Before a theatre performance, actors have rehearsed for months. Before the game, athletes have practiced countless hours of drills, skills, and plays. Before the dinner party, the caterer works to develop dishes and taste-test recipes in search of perfect pairings. Writers, too, must take the time to rehearse, practice, and develop their skills at writing craft-fully and skilfully. So provide opportunities for students to play, explore, be adventurous, and take risks with their writing, free of censure and grading.

When teaching specific craft techniques (effective lead sentences, alliteration, onomatopoeia, magic of three, brand names, verb and adverb pairings, effective endings, personification, hyperbole, repetition, proper nouns, using illuminating examples, adding a statistic, inserting a quote, etc.), encourage developing writers to play with the technique long before you ask them to independently include it in their own writing. Draw students' attention to a craft technique in a mentor text, then isolate it and use it as the model to emulate. Next, ask students to give it a go and freely muck around with the new technique in their Writer's Notebooks. By focusing on one small aspect of the writing, you release students from the multitude of demands that weigh them down when they are crafting an entire piece of text. As ideas begin to flow and their pencils fly across the page, harness this writing energy and have students flood the room with their writing. In our classroom, students can be seen perched on their knees in their chairs with arms waving in the air, eager to share. Our job as teachers is simply to listen and "Oooh" and "Aaah." You might even ask to borrow their words and note them in your own Writer's Notebook or record them on a Lines That Linger anchor chart. This organic sharing will bring joy, laughter, and levity to your writing community.

The Habit of Goal-Setting

Goals drive our thoughts, actions, and efforts. Think about a personal goal you have. It can be as simple as packing a healthy lunch each day or as grand as hiking to Machu Picchu and floating down the Amazon River (which we will be doing July 2021). Consider the commitment, planning, and sacrifices you may have to make to achieve your goal. It takes effort and energy, determination and perseverance to reach any goal. In our classrooms it is no different. We craft many goals with our students: learning skills, behavior, subject-area expectations, and more. However, when these goals are set without being monitored by student or teacher, it's not a surprise that they are rarely met. When setting goals with students, we cannot adopt the crockpot mentality of setting them and forgetting them. We must support students as they set, monitor, and reflect on their goals.

In our writing classrooms, we want to create the habit of setting specific, manageable goals. But it's been our experience that students have difficulty doing this when left to their own devices. How often have you witnessed a student draft a writing goal that is incredibly vague: *write longer stories; use harder words; print neater*? Or goals might be totally unrealistic: *Write a chapter book*. These ineffective goals stem from our students' lack of awareness of the many elements that contribute to a person being a passionate and proficient writer. They are not mindful of their own strengths and areas of need as writers, which in turn leads them to randomly formulate goals that are vague and unrealistic. Students seem to pull these goals from out of thin air, eagerly set them, and quickly forget them. However, if you have invested time in developing the first three habits—Find, Plan, and Act—then you have frontloaded the knowledge students need to be able to craft a specific goal.

Students will
- work collaboratively to build an anchor chart that outlines characteristics of a passionate and proficient writer

Passionate/Proficient Writer Anchor Chart

We have worked diligently to reveal the habits of authentic writers to our students through the Find, Plan, and Act activities. Now is the time to discover what students have internalized and committed to memory. Prepare yourself to be impressed!

1. Begin by asking your students to think about the following prompt: *What characteristics make a passionate and proficient writer?* Encourage students to share their thinking with an elbow partner.
2. Once they have had an opportunity to brainstorm together, have students share their ideas while you record their thinking on chart paper.

Sample Passionate and Proficient Writers Anchor Chart

Passionate Writers…	Proficient Writers…
<ul><li>are able to sense which topics and ideas have potential</li><li>are keenly observant of their surroundings, using it for writing inspiration, and jot down their ideas</li><li>are mindful of their writing territories (topics they know about, care about, and or wonder about)</li><li>embrace their Writer's Notebook as an essential tool in their writing life</li><li>know which text types they enjoy using and frequently explore the features and characteristics</li><li>dedicate specific times in their day for writing to develop stamina</li><li>have favorite spaces and places at school and home to write</li><li>have favorite tools to write with</li><li>talk about their writing with other authors</li><li>are eager to share their writing with their classmates, friends and family, community</li><li>understand the reciprocal nature between reading and writing</li><li>use other authors' work as inspiration</li><li>are eager to write</li></ul>	<ul><li>generate and develop ideas</li><li>select formats based on purpose and audience</li><li>use a variety of formats to communicate</li><li>know that writing is thinking on paper</li><li>carry on an inner conversation while they write</li><li>use the writing process to compose text</li><li>understand the various writing traits and features that writers use to draft text (Ideas, Organization, Sentence Fluency, Word Choice, Descriptive Devices, Voice, Craft Techniques, Format Features, etc.)</li><li>identify writing craft technique preferences</li><li>use resources (dictionary and thesaurus)</li><li>use feedback to elevate the quality of their writing</li><li>understand the value of revision</li><li>edit their work carefully</li><li>understand the role of structure in composing text (Fiction: characters, setting, plot, problem/solution; Nonfiction: main idea, supporting details)</li></ul>

This list is by no means an exhaustive one. Your students will likely come up with many more ideas linked to writing habits, traits, features, skills, strategies, craft techniques, the writing process, etc.

Setting a Writing Goal

Students will
- watch you model setting a specific and manageable writing goal connected to a plan of action and indicators of success, using the previously co-constructed anchor chart

Modeling the creation of specific and manageable goals that match the writers in the room is imperative. It reveals to students the thinking and reflection that must be put into creating an appropriate goal. So demonstrate the thought process a writer goes through when crafting a fitting goal.

1. Start by modeling your own goal using the co-constructed Passionate/Proficient Writer anchor chart from page 79:

    Yesterday we created this extensive anchor chart that outlines all the things we know a passionate, proficient writer does. But to be honest, I'm not sure I do all those things consistently and thoughtfully.

    (At this point you might take time with your class to tease out what "consistently" and "thoughtfully" mean to them.)

    So today I want to read the chart and identify all the things I think I do consistently and thoughtfully.

    (Place a colored sticky note beside each characteristic that describes you as a writer on the anchor chart. As you examine the characteristics, think out loud and justify your *Yeses* and your *Nos*.)

    For example, I always carry my Thought Jot book in my purse or bag to record ideas for writing. When I notice something that intrigues me or I find surprising, I jot it down. You never know where an idea might emerge! I also love to keep lists of favorite words, unique words, or quotes that speak to me in some way. They provide inspiration for my writing. As well, if you were to walk into my book room you would find my Writer's Notebook on my desk. This is the place where I do most of my writing, where I am surrounded by writing inspiration—the books and authors I love and whose writing I admire and read often. My thesaurus, rhyming dictionary, and verb dictionary are all within arm's reach.

    On the other hand, when I look at these lists further, I notice it says a writer uses a variety of craft techniques. Thinking about this, I realize that I certainly have my preferences and use them frequently: magic of three, alliteration, sensory details. I wonder, though, how my writing might improve if I used a wider variety of craft. For example, I rarely use similes, personification, and onomatopoeia. Using these techniques could be a goal for me. Another thing I notice is that share my writing with students but I rarely make it public beyond the classroom. Sharing my writing with my family or posting it on the bulletin board in the school corridor would make me a more contributing member to our classroom writing community and expand my writing audience.

    This think-aloud process is vital to making students understand the inner dialogue we want them to have as they reflect on themselves as writers. This information will be used to set their own writing goal.

2. Distribute copies of the anchor chart for individual students to use as a tool to reflect on their own writer characteristics. Direct students to pencil a checkmark beside the characteristics they demonstrate consistently and thoughtfully, while pencilling a star beside two characteristics they think make an appropriate goal.

3. Gather students so that they can watch closely as you model creating a plan of action for a goal that is specific and manageable:

As I've mentioned, I think I skilfully use the craft techniques of magic of three, alliteration, and sensory details. I think I'm good at these techniques because I have played with them loads of times in my writing. Now, I think it's time to broaden my repertoire, to spice up my writing with new techniques. Similes, personification, and onomatopoeia would all add a boost to the creativity of my work. So I am going to set the following goal: Play with similes, personification, and onomatopoeia in my writing.

4. Note that this is where wheels often fall off the bus. Students typically do not devise a plan of action. They don't think through the specific steps they need to take to meet their goal. Continue to specify your plan of action:

   I think the perfect place to start to play around with these techniques is in my Writer's Notebook. I am going to read like a writer—on the look out for these techniques being used in the texts I am reading. To inspire me, I will keep a list in my Writer's Notebook of examples that really pop out at me. And when I'm drafting, I can play with these techniques in the margin to determine which one sounds best to my ear. I will commit to share one piece with you in the author's chair over the next couple of weeks and will ask you to pay attention to my use of these craft devices.

Extension

You need to support each student in setting an appropriate, specific, and manageable goal with a concrete plan of action. This requires you to sit one-on-one and conference with each student. Working alongside students will pay huge dividends in getting to know the writers in your class, seeing connections between them, planning your writing mini-lessons, and, most importantly, setting up your writers for success. We acknowledge that these writing conferences will take time. But without this essential step to support developing writers, you will end up with a crockpot of unmet goals that students will set and forget. To ensure this doesn't happen, check in frequently with writers to monitor their progress; see page 85 for a Writing Goal bookmark that will serve as a tool to remind them daily of their goal. As students develop the habit of setting goals, achieving them, and drafting new ones, you might find that the level of support students require of you decreases.

Format Flea-Market Finds

Text: Format: Features:	Text: Format: Features:	Text: Format: Features:	Text: Format: Features:	Text: Format: Features:
Text: Format: Features:	Text: Format: Features:	Text: Format: Features:	Text: Format: Features:	Text: Format: Features:

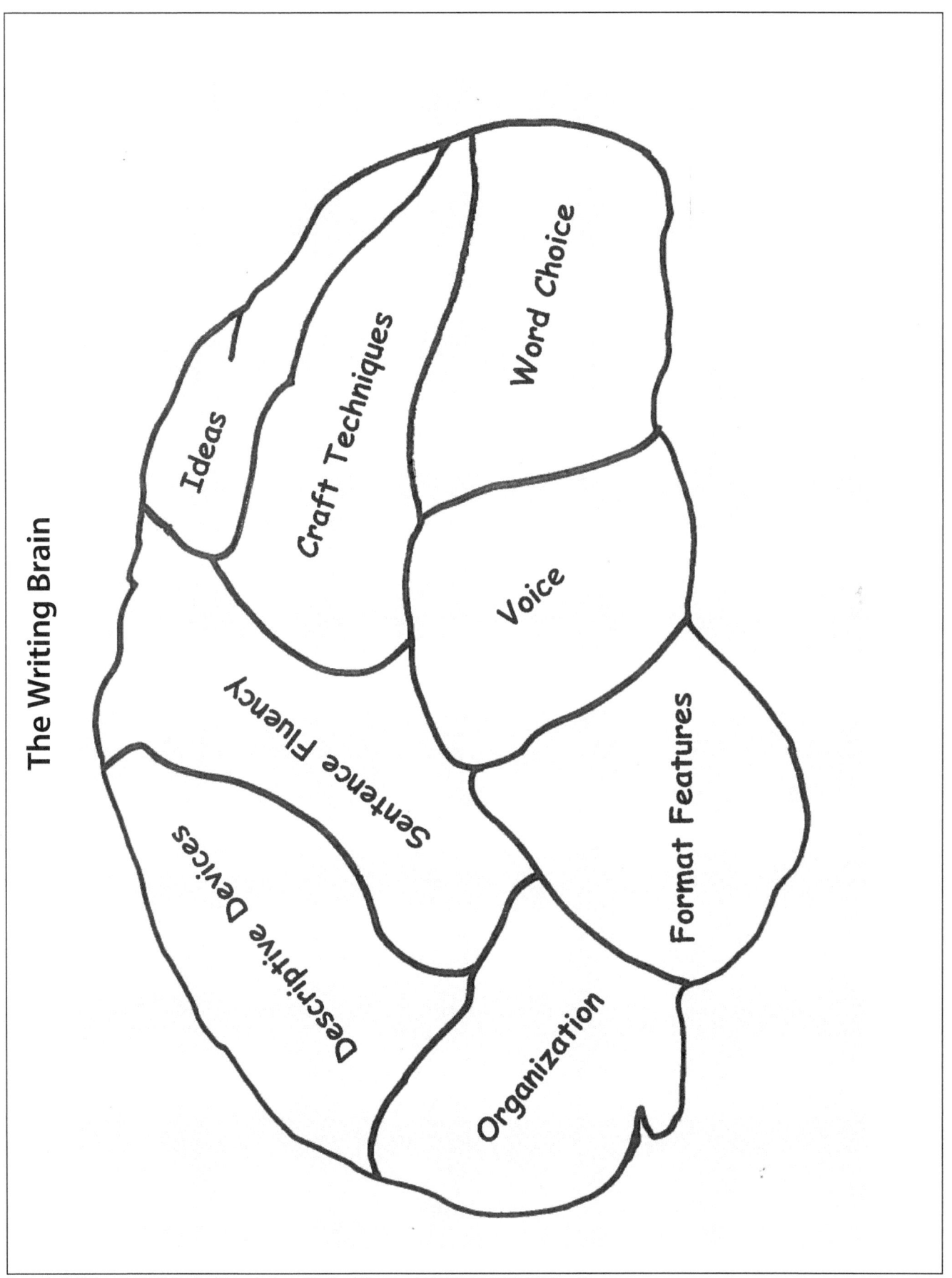

My Writing Brain

Name: _____

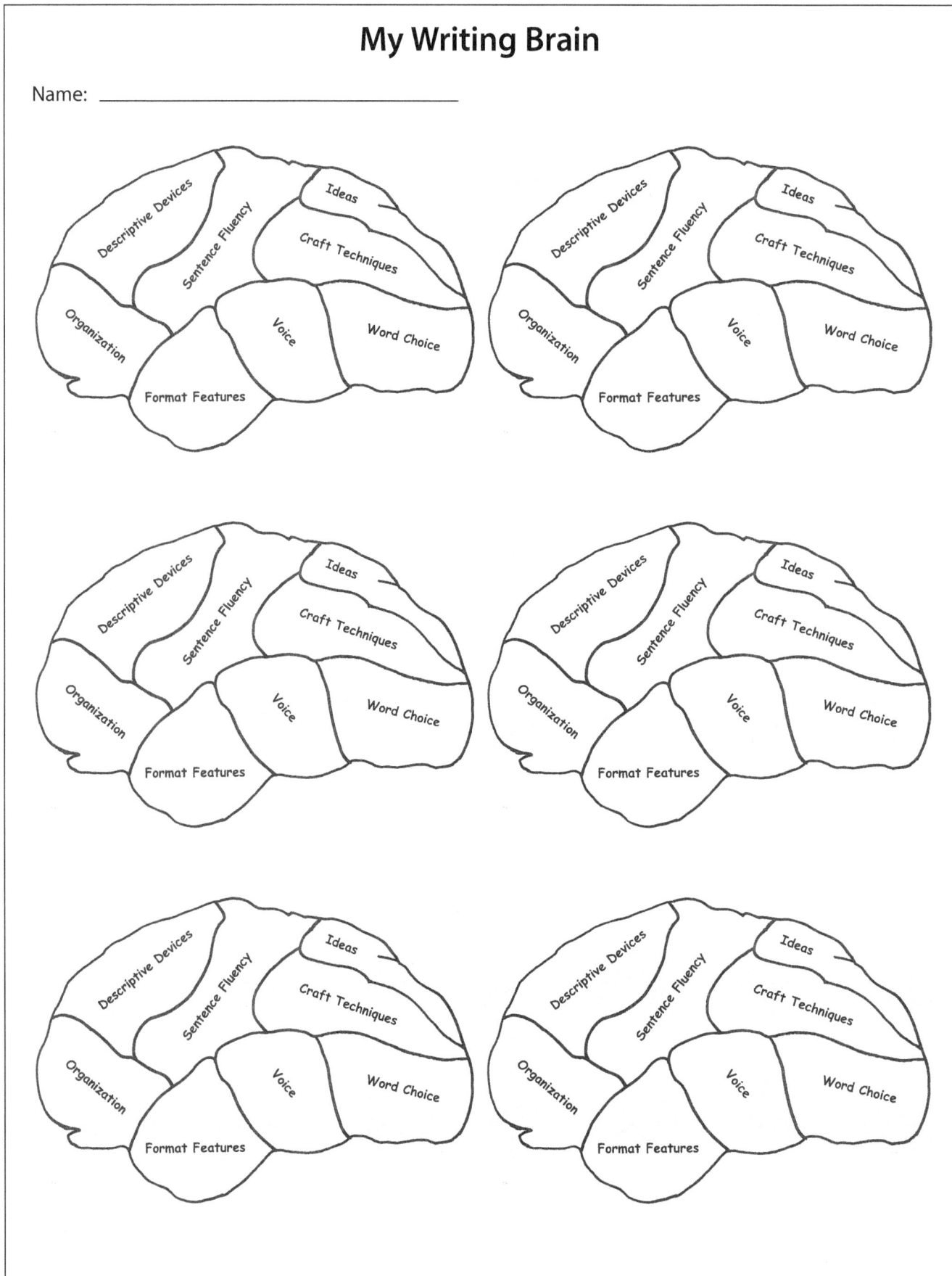

Writing Goal Bookmark

Habits of a Writer

FIND ideas.

PLAN forms and formats for writing.

ACT as a writer by reading, thinking, talking, and sharing what you have written.

SET writing goals.

_____'s Writing Goal:

To become a better writer, I will…

_____

_____

_____

_____

_____

Habits of a Writer

FIND ideas.

PLAN forms and formats for writing.

ACT as a writer by reading, thinking, talking, and sharing what you have written.

SET writing goals.

_____'s Writing Goal:

To become a better writer, I will…

_____

_____

_____

_____

_____

Fourth Step: Make the *Why* of Writing Visible

5

You open the car door, sit in the seat and buckle up. It's an automatic action that takes very little thinking. But a few decades ago, most did not consider wearing seat belts when operating or riding in a motor vehicle. The strap was seen as uncomfortable and restrictive, and it reduced the mobility of passengers. So why wear it? Widespread government campaigns were undertaken to increase knowledge and understanding of the critical safety effects of seat belts. An onslaught of information was blasted at drivers and passengers; research, statistics, billboards, commercials, PSAs, personal testimonials, and celebrity endorsements all worked together to change the mindset of North Americans. Seat belt laws ensured that everyone was using this life-saving device. In the 21st century, it's considered unheard of and negligent to not buckle up and ensure that everyone is safely fastened in.

In education we're no different from drivers and passengers. To shift our thinking and change our practice, the *why* needs to be made clearly visible. We need to be swayed, won over, and convinced. For educators, it takes

- educational research
- personal testimonials of colleagues and friends
- presenter power
- literacy-leader name-dropping

Together these all work to shift our thinking and change our practice by making the *why* visible.

Why Write?

As classroom teachers, we are faced with the challenge of having to sway, persuade, and convince our students that writing is indeed a worthwhile activity. We have to make the *why* visible to them so that they shift their thinking, change their beliefs, and adopt new habits. Typically, without providing any evidence or justification for the statement, we have merely told students that writing is important and expected them to believe us. Is it any surprise that many students do not believe that writing is important and fail to see the point in becoming proficient and passionate writers? We need to provide students with evidence that they can understand and relate to if we want to change their attitude. Additionally, as lead writers, we must continually deconstruct the vague message that writing is beneficial into specific and tangible explanations that answer the question "Why write?"

Students benefit from hearing the sales pitch from the lead writer in the room. We are in a prime position to passionately communicate to them the range of reasons that writing is important, valuable, and beneficial to them. But we cannot do this by merely telling; we must create learning experiences that show them. Back in 2002, Kelly Gallagher did just that for middle- and high-school students with reading. Based on nine real-world reading reasons, he created lessons to show and tell his students why being a reader is imperative. His work inspired us to reflect on how we could convey a more age-appropriate message to our younger students about writing. Through our work in classrooms these writing reasons have emerged year after year:

- We write to express our thoughts and feelings.
- We write to record and document memories.
- We write for pleasure and enjoyment.
- We write to clarify our thinking and to share knowledge and experiences.
- We write to become better writers.
- We write to become more appreciative readers.
- We write to share valuable life lessons.
- We write to describe, explain, entertain, and persuade.

> Every lesson speaks to a number of reasons to write. Students have a very narrow perception of why writing is important. We need to expand their lens; each lesson will help students see the big picture to focus on the many motives for writing.

Chocolate chip cookies and a glass of milk; sandy beach and SPF 30; salty chips and creamy dip; movies and buttery popcorn; cold winter days and a warm crackling fire—some things naturally seem to go together, and the benefits of writing are no different. They overlap, intertwine, and genuinely reinforce one other. It's impossible to address one writing reason without exalting another. We cannot teach them in isolation, nor do we need to.

> *Mary*
>
> When I wrote about the time I tackled my fear of riding the Ghoster Coaster at Canada's Wonderland with my young daughter Jennifer in tow, I wrote the piece to record and document a memory. Other reasons and benefits of drafting this piece I discovered were:
> - I was able to express my thoughts and feelings.
> - I shared my knowledge and experience of a significant event in my life and reflected on a valuable life lesson I learned.

Giving the Gift of Writing

In our experience, students see writing as anything but a gift. They view it as a chore, a task, an assignment, a job to be done. They have to discover that writing provides a wealth of life-long emotional, creative, and intellectual benefits. So let's remove the wrapping and expose the powerful gift inside.

1. Gather items and place them in a large gift bag: pencil, pen, marker, lined paper, journal, postcard, sticky notes, diary, calendar, Writer's Notebook,

> Students will
> - begin to identify the various reasons to write (emotional, creative, and intellectual)

recipe cards, small whiteboard, thesaurus, dictionary, etc. Fill the top of the bag with sheets of colored tissue paper to create a beautiful presentation.
2. Place the bag front and centre in the classroom where students cannot miss it.
3. Invite students to gather around as you slowly remove one item from the bag at a time. As you reveal each item, encourage students to think privately and silently why these items have been collected into one bag and how they are connected.
4. Once all the items have been laid out before them, have students turn and talk with a partner to discuss the possible connection between all the items and attempt to encapsulate the connection into a single word.
5. Have students share their thinking with the larger group. Responses will likely include: *writing, tools, resources, communication*.
6. Once students have shared their initial thoughts, pose the question: *What is the purpose of writing tools?* Be sure to record student responses on an anchor chart: *to record, to document, to remember, to communicate, to share information, to create, to reflect, to spell, to expand our vocabulary*, etc.
7. Share with students why you put all these items into a gift bag:

> *I chose to place these writing tools in a gift bag because I believe that writing truly is a gift. Without the ability to write, we wouldn't be able to record our memories, document our thinking, remember our experiences, express our thoughts and feelings, share our knowledge with others, and create magical stories to entertain one another. Writing is wonderful gift!*

Extension

Over the next number of days, mindfully select read-alouds that will address various writing reasons. Anything that moves you, makes you laugh, teaches you something, touches your heart, or compels you to act is a text worth sharing. After you have read each text, ask students to answer the following questions: *Why do you think the author choose to write this book? What do you think the author's purpose or reason for writing was?* Track student thinking on a chart linked to the title of the text.

Writing to Express Thoughts and Feelings

Hallmark, Carlton, and Papyrus have cornered the market on greeting cards. You name it, there is a card for it. We merely need to peruse the wide variety until we find the one that expresses our thoughts, feelings, and sentiments; then we pay a king's ransom for the folded piece of decorated card stock and sign it! How many of those expensive pieces of paper end up being pitched in the garbage can? Consider being gifted a greeting card with a personal heartfelt message inscribed within. The writing turns the card into something that is treasured, reread, and kept as a keepsake.

Committing our thoughts and feelings to paper seems to have become a forgotten art. We have robbed ourselves the experience of contemplating, reflecting, and releasing our emotions onto the page. This type of expressive writing has loads of benefits and is truly cathartic. Research has shown that it
- helps us connect with others
- benefits our emotional well-being

For all lessons in this chapter, students will
- begin to identify the various reasons to write (express thoughts and feelings, clarify thinking and ideas, record and document a memory, share valuable life lessons, etc.)

It's essential that we provide time and space for students to express their thoughts and feelings on paper.

- improves immune function and reduces health complaints
- builds a sense of community
- helps us understand and manage our emotions
- supports us in developing positive relationships
- increases our ability to cope with life challenges

(Graves, 1994; Pennebaker in Smith, n.d.; Pennebaker, Barger & Tiebout in Smith, n.d.; Pennebaker, Kiecolt-Glaser & Glaser in Smith, n.d.)

Bursting Onto the Page

Have you ever heard the expression "You'll feel better if you talk about it"? Well, we believe you'll feel better if you write about. Happy, excited, overwhelmed, nervous, joyful, elated, crushed, frustrated—you name it, we feel it and it's cathartic to express it in writing. As Graves says, writing helps us define our feelings and connects us to others (1994). Ann Lamott concurs that writing "is about some of our deepest needs: our need to be visible, to be heard, our need to make sense of our lives, to wake up and grow and belong" (1994, p. 19).

Students will
- relate images of exploding natural wonders to the feeling they experience when they release their thoughts and emotions in writing
- begin to identify the various reasons to write (express thoughts and feelings, record and document a memory, share an experience, clarify thinking and ideas, etc.)

1. Gather a variety of images of things that are about to burst or explode:
   - pot boiling over
   - volcano about to erupt
   - jack-in-the-box
   - dam about to burst
   - balloon with a pin near it
   - confetti launcher
   - baseball about to hit a window

2. Prominently display the images around the room and have students travel to view them. Encourage them to think about what the images have in common. Students will be eager to express that these images all depict things that are about to erupt, burst, release, explode, shatter, and rupture.

3. Pose the question:

   Have you ever felt like you were going to erupt, burst, release, explode, or shatter? Share with a partner a time you have felt one of these ways.

4. Once students have had an opportunity to share their thinking with a peer, have them express their ideas. For example, *I thought I was going to burst waiting in line to get on the roller coaster; My heart felt like it was going to shatter when my pet had to have surgery; I almost exploded when my brother broke my music box; I was erupting with excitement when I got my new bike;* etc.

5. Encourage students to record their experience/thinking/emotions on paper. As the lead writer, you need to do this as well!

6. Have students who are willing to share read their quick writes to the class.

7. Ask students to consider what the benefits of expressing their thoughts and feelings in writing have been for them.

Students will
- begin to identify the various reasons to write (express thoughts and feelings, clarify thinking and ideas, record and document a memory, share valuable life lessons, etc.)

Inside-Out Writing

Mary

Over the last several years, I have been coming to terms with my mother's journey into dementia, a crippling disease that steals the person you know and love away from you in front of your very eyes. Anger, frustration, sadness, guilt are just some of the emotions that have set up residence inside me. In attempting to process these emotions, I have turned to my Writer's

Writing to Express Thoughts and Feelings

> Notebook and allowed my varied thoughts and emotions to pour onto the page. At first this act enabled me to unburden myself of heavy emotions and led to a sense of release. But over time, I have written my way to a new understanding and perspective on this confusing situation. I arrived at the epiphany that I could live in a state of mourning what I have lost while my mother is still alive, or I could choose to be grateful and recognize what I still have. For example, my mother continues to be a teacher in a different capacity. No longer passing on her gifts of sewing, knitting, baking, and crafting, now she passes on her sense of wonder, her childlike ability to notice, marvel at, and be mesmerized by the natural world around her. She compels me to stop and notice a bird perched precariously on the feeder, greedily pecking at the sunflower seeds. She points with intent at the puffy white clouds floating across the blue sky and stares in awe. She gingerly caresses the soft petals of flowers as she walks in the courtyard of her long-term care home. These precious moments continue my mother's legacy of teaching, just in a different way.
>
> When reviewing my writing about my mother, I began to notice a preoccupation with all I was losing. I wondered if this contributed to my dwelling in sadness and grief. This prompted me to pause and reflect on what was still there. One day after a particularly difficult visit, I returned home and began to draft a list poem of what I had and simple pleasures I could still enjoy with my mother:
>
> > I can still hug you
> > I can still sit in quiet comfort with you
> > I can still tell you about my kids
> > I can still hear your laugh
> > I can still watch you demonstrate a mother's love with your baby
> > I can still see you perk up when I walk in the room
> > I can still see your smile
> > I can still hear you say "I love you too."
>
> From this writing that lets what is inside out, I gained a sense of clarity and perspective. I refused to let grief consume me, but rather chose to appreciate and enjoy what I still had. Writing about my mom allowed me to express my personal thoughts and feelings on paper, enabled me to record observations about my mother, allowed me to revisit and clarify my thinking and ideas—all leading to new understandings. That's the incredible power of writing.

Creating the conditions for students to engage in this type of personal, vulnerable, and courageous writing requires that we provide them with the time and space to do so. As a writing community, this occurs during free writing time in our Writer's Notebooks. Students must have places where they can personally journal and be honest with themselves, spaces where they can engage in writing that "scrapes the heart" (Fletcher, 1996).

Often a text we read aloud is a catalyst for this personal and private type of writing. For example after reading *Mum and Dad Glue* by Kes Gray, a number of students in Anne's class were compelled to write about their parents' separa-

If a student deems a piece of writing for their eyes only, tell them to fold the page over to ensure confidentiality.

tion and divorce; in Mary's classroom, a few students wrote of times they were unkind and hurtful to others after listening to the text *Each Kindness* by Jacqueline Woodson. Things that keep you awake at night, cause you to worry, and hurt your heart are things worth writing about. So let those thoughts and feelings out! When these powerful writing experiences occur on the page, take time to draw students' attention to benefits this writing has for them and draw connections to your Why Write anchor chart to make the value of writing transparent.

Writing to Record and Document Memories

> "Sometimes you never know the value of a moment until it becomes a memory."—Dr. Seuss

We are products of our past; our everyday experiences shape who we are. Our adventures, mishaps, joys, heartaches, and celebrations are abundant sources of writing potential. Often our students disregard and dismiss their lived experience as not being grand or exciting enough to be worthy of writing. How very wrong they are! Documenting and recording what, at first glance, seems small and trivial often yields riches. Our personal stories reveal our culture, history, life lessons, values, and beliefs.

When Anne talks about writing from a memory with students she is very upfront about the fact that, at the age of 42, she has a vast bank to draw from that allows an ease when asked to reminisce and reflect. This is a challenge for our younger writers, who do not have the sheer number of experiences—the cumulative number of birthdays, holidays, vacations, etc.—to tap into. However, they have lived; they do have memories and experiences that deserve to be documented. Your role as the lead writer is to make transparent the benefits of reflecting on memories and recording them with as much authentic detail as possible. In doing so, we reminisce, relive, rejoice, review, reaffirm, and, consequently, gain perspective and wisdom. So provide opportunities for students to reminisce about their past in writing and also to commit things to memory by writing about events that have more recently occurred. Both of these writing acts validate our stories, showing that they matter and need to be voiced.

> Chapter 3 discusses that having your students mine their lives for writing ideas is a worthwhile and valuable task. The lessons here continue to build on the work you have already done and shine a light on this writing reason.

Memories Written to Music

> *Anne*
>
> I am a huge country music fan. My fascination with this strain of music stems from my father's love of this genre and the remarkable ability of the lyrics to tell a story in a heartfelt and compelling way. Country music is filled with songs that encapsulate a memory and teach life lessons—all in just under four minutes!

In *Genre Connections*, Tanny McGregor offers a list of songs, essentially memoirs, that she uses to teach this type of writing, and we, too, have used songs to stimulate memory writing in our students. Here is a list of some of Anne's country music favorites:

"Coat of Many Colors" by Dolly Parton
"Coal Miner's Daughter" by Loretta Lynn
"Lessons Learned" by Tracy Lawrence

"I Thought He Walked on Water" by Randy Travis
"In Color" by Jamey Johnson
"Sixteen" by Thomas Rhett

We encourage you to consider using songs to highlight this benefit of writing; i.e., to record and document memories. The age and grade of students you teach will determine your own selection. So listen, reflect, talk, and then write down memories ignited by the song.

Write that Down

> *Mary*
>
> Zackery pulled out the resealable bag from the recesses of his desk and held it up for all to see, exclaiming, "What is this?" The room erupted into a chorus of *Ewww!*'s and *Disgusting!*'s. He carried the bag across the room with his arm outstretched as if afraid its moss-green contents would come to life and attack him. The rest of the class watched in horror as a cloud puffed up from the garbage pail when it hit the bottom. We all began to ponder and question what it had at one time been: a bologna sandwich, a chicken wrap, a bunch of grapes? When the dust finally settled, I exclaimed to students, "Get out your Writer's Notebooks and write this memorable moment down." For the remainder of the year, each and every time Zachary cleaned out his desk, the students braced themselves and watched in anticipation for what might emerge.

Every classroom is filled to the brim with moments that should be written down for posterity's sake: the fart that rocked the silent room; the time the class was moved to tears while reading *Hana's Suitcase*; the day the vial of ants were being transferred to the ant farm and the refrigeration had not done its work; skating as a class to "The Locomotion" at the nearby arena. Training our students to recognize and record these daily events requires time and deliberate intention on our part. We need to stop the action in the room, grab our notebooks, and jot down this writing gold. In time, students will naturally adopt this habit and, without direction, record memorable moments in their notebooks for future writing.

Writing for Pleasure and Enjoyment

Reading and writing are two sides of the same coin. In reading we consume text; in writing we produce it. In reading we inhale text; in writing we exhale. In reading we receive; in writing we give. Recognizing this relationship allows us to investigate an author's purpose for writing.

Many authors write to entertain and to give pleasure and enjoyment to their audience. By intentionally selecting read-alouds that are filled with fun and humor, you send the message to students that writing has a lighter side and that not all texts we craft are serious. Charles Dickens said it best: "There is nothing in the world more irresistibly contagious as laughter and good humor." Studies have shown that laughter can decrease stress, reduce anxiety, help you sleep better, burn calories, and release endorphins, while increasing overall happiness. Using mentor texts that invoke pleasure is essential to demonstrate one reason that we write is for the pleasure and enjoyment of both the writer and the reader.

Texts that Tickle

Seek out books that will lead to laugh-out-loud moments for you and your students. Your school librarian can point you in the direction of authors whose books overflow with humor. Our go-to authors include Mélanie Watt, Robert Munsch, Mo Willems, Shel Silverstein, and Dav Pilkey. As well, some notable titles that tickle our funny bones:

Drew Daywalt, *The Day the Crayons Quit*
David Ezra Stein, *Interrupting Chicken*
Heather Hartt-Sussman, *Nana's Getting Married*
Jason Lefebvre, *Too Much Glue*

With older students, consider using *Guys Read—Funny Business* edited by Jon Scieszka or *Chicken Soup for the Kid's Soul: 101 Stories of Courage, Hope and Laughter* by Jack Canfield and Mark Victor Hansen, or even fractured fairy tales to inject laughter into your classroom. These stories will have your students rolling in laughter and appreciating that one of the main reasons we write is to give pleasure and enjoyment to our audience.

The Enjoyment Factor

Anne's dad loves to go the horse races; her mom loves to read and to scratch lottery tickets. Mary's son Mark is obsessed with soccer and her husband Peter is an avid golfer. Each of these family members has activities they derive pleasure and enjoyment from. And I bet you do, too! It's necessary that our developing writers come to know that authors derive joy and delight from the act of writing and from the responses they receive from readers.

Fostering connections between students and the authors they read and enjoy is a great place to start. Be sure to track the names of the authors students read independently and ones they have enjoyed during class read-alouds. Once you have a few names, don't be afraid to reach out and make a connection with them via social media or email. Most authors are open to receiving comments and questions from readers via Twitter and personal email. Many authors offer school visits that are engaging and entertaining to audiences of all ages; others are happy to connect with readers via Skype or Zoom for a nominal fee.

> *Mary*
>
> I fondly remember my class writing fan letters to Robert Munsch and in return receiving a thoughtful note, a poster, and an unpublished manuscript with his handwritten revisions all over it. The students were excited to receive such a remarkable gift.

> *Anne*
>
> I recall having acclaimed Canadian authors Barbara Reid, Maxine Trottier, Michael Wade, Eric Walters, and Kevin Sylvester visit schools I taught at to speak to students. These visits were priceless injections of energy for developing writers. Hearing first-hand where great writers get story ideas and about their writing process, and then having them read their writing aloud, is a captivating experience.

It is a unique experience for students to meet an author whose stories have had an impact on them and to hear right from their mouth the pleasure and enjoyment they receive from writing text for others. When authors visit, prepare your students in advance to ask pointed questions at the end of a presentation, such as
- What are the benefits you get from writing?
- What types of habits and routines do you have as an author?
- Why is it important for you to connect with readers?

Students sometimes have the chance to witness the impact their comments, praise, and accolades have on the author themselves. The Forest of Reading run by the Ontario Library Association (and similar reading programs) foster this appreciation of authors and the connection between writers and their young fans. At the Festival of Trees event, students are able to attend author-led workshops and join the long lines to meet their favorite writers. It's touching to watch students' eager faces as they reach the front of the line, have a few words with their hero, snap a selfie, and get their book signed. A symbiotic relationship exists between authors and readers, built on pleasure and enjoyment. We work toward students coming to experience similar feelings of fulfilment and happiness from sharing their writing, just as published writers do.

Writing to Clarify Thinking and to Share Knowledge and Experiences

Judy Willis (2017) attests:

> Writing promotes the brain's attentive focus to class work and homework, promotes long-term memory, illuminates patterns… gives the brain time for reflection, and… is a source of conceptual development and stimulus of the brain's highest cognition.

When we provide opportunities for students to clarify their thinking, they develop greater confidence in the content and can even become authorities on the subject.

Every classroom has these resident experts, students who know anything and everything you ever want to know about dinosaurs, rocks, skateboarding, beading, weather, lacrosse, or life in another country. They use every chance they can to inject a piece of trivia on their passion topic into classroom conversations. These experts long to educate, inform, and excite anyone willing to listen to their fun facts. I'm sure you can recall a student or two who entertained you while on yard duty with their flood of knowledge. Each student in your class has passions, interests and pockets of knowledge that need to be released into your learning community. They also are filled to the brim with curiosities that you must provide time for them to explore and opportunities for them to share new discoveries. Topics of investigation are not merely determined by the curriculum or teacher; rather, student curiosity and enthusiasm drive classroom conversation, research, and, above all, topics for writing. When students are given the authority to choose their own topics, we honor their curiosity, questions, and wonderings. We empower them to follow their interests, share what they know, and inquire further. Let the topic-finding begin!

Triple-C Card

Two of the greatest sources of information about topics students feel capable and confident writing on are the Interest Inventory (see page 31) and the Authority List (see page 38). These activities reveal areas of knowledge and experience that students can effortlessly tap into for writing. Often, as teachers, we don't capitalize on the wealth of possibilities for writing these tools lead us to. In turn, students overlook what they know, and need to be reminded that most authors write from a place of knowing. Identifying and recording a list of topics students are curious, capable, and confident writing about is a great way to keep their expertise at the forefront and spark writing filled with voice. The Triple-C Card (see template on page 103) is a quick and easy way for students to track these kernels of knowledge and experience from their Interest Inventory and Authority List. Directing student's attention to their card is a powerful reminder that they have topics which are familiar and exciting for them.

> As a teacher–model creating your own Triple-C Card, be mindful of recording things you know about and things you want to know more about.

Anne

My Triple-C Card usually includes:
- Elephants
- Travel
- Importance of access to clean water
- Baking
- Selling books to students
- the Victorian Era
- Country music

Resident Experts

Our classrooms are filled with students who are unofficial experts on the Toronto Maple Leafs, Minecraft, the boyband BTS, Medieval Times, and Canadian figure-skating legends Tessa Virtue and Scott Moir. Let's exploit these knowledgeable others by recording and tracking their areas of expertise.

1. Create a grid on chart paper, ensuring there is one box for each student in your class. Be sure to have ample space in the box to document their areas of expertise.
2. Record student names alphabetically.
3. We have experienced the greatest success with this activity by constructing the chart during one-on-one conferences with students. Pose the question: "Tell me, what are a few things you think you have a fair amount of prior knowledge about?"
4. Record student responses immediately on the chart.

5. Once you have had an opportunity to conference with all students, expose the expertise within the room with a sense of excitement and delight.

Students will be awe-inspired to discover the amount of knowledge within the room that they can access and tap into when writing, as well as connections they share with peers. Be sure to frequently draw students' attention to the chart as a source of information for their writing, intentionally integrate student expert knowledge into modeled writing lessons, and add to the chart as new expertise emerges throughout the year. Let's face it, writers write about what they know!

Writing-in-the-Real-World Interview

Students will
- interview a parent or guardian to uncover the purposeful writing they do related to their work

Oh, how the world has changed! Telecommunications have significantly affected the workforce. Mary recalls the days of old when there was no such thing as email in the workplace. Information that needed to be shared on the job occurred predominantly in face-to-face conversations; now communications bombard our email inboxes. The number of people who currently work remotely also has increased, putting an emphasis on written communication. In the current world of work, the demand for employees to record information, prepare written documents, and respond in writing to communications are frequent daily occurrences. Many jobs rely on employees to communicate articulately and effectively with coworkers via the written medium at an incredible rate.

We wonder if students are aware that the majority of jobs require and value proficient written communication skills. Do they have misconceptions that need to be corrected regarding the writing demands of the workplace? Address these issues head-on by having students interview a parent, guardian, or relative to uncover the writing requirements of their chosen profession. No need to make this a formal or labor-intensive activity.

1. Have students record the guiding question in their planner (*Can you tell me about the types of writing you need to do for your job?*) and provide each student with a lined sticky note to record their findings.
2. The next day, students share the results of their interview in small groups. Be sure to highlight the vast array of jobs held by interviewees and the many ways employees are required to be capable and proficient writers.

Extension

Consider inviting various school employees into the classroom to share the writing demands of their job: custodian, school counsellor, speech pathologist, Learning Coordinator for Technology, school community police officer, facility services workers, attendance counsellor, etc. Or consider having community members come in to your classroom to share the writing demands of their job.

List the Learning

Students will
- document the new information and understanding they acquire from reading a text

One of the fundamental gifts we receive from the writing of others is knowledge. Consider this, if writers never recorded what they know, what would *we* know?! If we never read, we wouldn't know that researchers have discovered that some aquatic turtles breathe through their butts! If we never read, we wouldn't know that more than 5,000 objects were discovered in Tutankhamun's tomb, including chariots, model boats, canopic jars, chairs, and paintings. If we never read, we wouldn't know Canadian James Naismith created the sport of basketball. So let's celebrate the source and track the new learning.

1. For this read-aloud, be explicit that the purpose of the reading is to recognize the vast amount of information and understandings we will gain from a particular text:

   Today I am excited to share with you an excerpt from the book Military Animals *by Laurie Calkhoven. While I read aloud I am going to ask you to track and document all the information that is new to you. At the end, I will be asking you to share your new knowledge with your classmates.*

2. When reading, keep in mind that the knowledge students gain will be both right-there, put-your-finger-on-it knowledge and enduring understandings of the big ideas that cannot be found directly on the page.
3. After reading, record a piece of new information/knowledge gained by each student. Be sure to identify each student's name beside their new nugget of knowledge. If more than one student has the same nugget, record both names.
4. Sum up by exclaiming, "The more you read, the more you know. Authors enlighten, inform, and educate us! What a reason to write."

Extension

As students publish their own informative pieces throughout the year, be sure to have them exchange their reports, newspaper articles, two-page spreads, biographies, etc. with their peers. Harness the authentic writing from within the classroom and have readers acknowledge the new learning they acquired from reading texts written by their classmates.

Using My Voice

Students will
- investigate various websites to build their background knowledge about current issues effecting our world
- clarify their thinking about issues and be compelled to inform, persuade, and influence others

"An educated, enlightened and informed population is one of the surest ways of promoting the health of a democracy" — Nelson Mandela, Speech Given at St. John's School, Johannesburg

As teachers, we need to create moments to inform young minds about events and situations currently facing our world. We are fortunate that many age-appropriate websites are just a click away. The following sites let our students access timely and informative content: *Wonderopolis, DOGO News, Time For Kids, Teaching Kids News, Scholastic News,* and *PBS NEWSHOUR EXTRA* (Grades 7–12). Or you might check out magazines such as *Currents4Kids* (Grades 3 and up) and *What in the World*? from Lesplan Educational Services, and *Action* and *Scope* from Scholastic. Each of these sources provides an abundance of news on a variety of subjects: current events, science, social studies, sports, arts, etc. Infuse your classroom with news, tapping into your students' innate curiosity to know more about their world.

At first, you will need to sniff out the news, draw students' attention to these websites/magazines, and provide the time and space to share these articles in class. But before long, your students' insatiable desire to know more about their world will compel them to seek out the news on their own; all you need to provide is the time, access, and validation. To clearly communicate the value and importance of being an informed citizen, sharing and discussion of current news events must happen on a weekly basis. As news stories are shared, use these prompts: *What new information have we added to our background knowledge? Why is it important that we know about this?*

For example, in 2019–2020, we were inundated with heart-breaking images and news stories regarding the devastating bushfires that spread across Australia. Reports indicated that millions of animals died, hundreds of thousands of people were evacuated, and countless fire fighters descended on the country from around the world to aid in relief efforts. Many news organizations and researchers cited climate change as one of the main factors in this disaster. Conversations among students focused on this event and various environmental issues involved. Many students were filled with compassion for the people and animals of the country, and longed to act, but needed guidance and support to channel their knowledge of the issue into doable action.

As Martin Luther said "If you want to change the world, pick up your pen and write." So when our students are disturbed, concerned, troubled, inspired, stirred, or moved by a particular issue, event, or problem we encourage them to write! Through this worthwhile action, students develop their ideas, clarify their thinking, and come to know that, as citizens, they have a responsibility to speak up and share their thoughts. They must know that their voice has value, that it matters and needs to be inserted into the conversation about local, national, and global issues. Just look at the power of Greta Thunberg's voice on the climate change debate.

Consider reading aloud excerpts from books to inspire and motivate students in your class to use their voice and pen to make change in our world for the better. Some good examples:

Nancy Runstedler, *Pay it Forward Kids: Small Acts, Big Change*
Janet Wilson, *One Peace: True Stories of Young Activists*
Janet Wilson, *Our Rights: How Kids are Changing the World*
Janet Wilson, *Our Earth: How Kids are Saving the Planet*
Janet Wilson, *Our Heroes: How Kids are Making a Difference*
Janet Wilson, *Our Future: How Kids are Taking Action*

Animal rights, homelessness, lack of access to clean water in First Nations communities, recycling, plastic in our oceans, child labor—name an issue and it will fire up your students to become activists! Provide opportunities and outlets for writers to express themselves in letters, articles, editorials, emails, announcements, posters, infographics, poems, opinion pieces, etc. When our students have something to say, let them be heard.

Writing to Become a Better Writer

In our classrooms, we make the case that students need plenty of time to invest in reading each day. They must develop the stamina and endurance to stay with a text and to go deep. Extended reading opportunities are essential for students to engage with the text, get swept away in the storyline, hold the narrative, absorb the content, and, above all, derive enjoyment from this activity. Without stamina, readers are not able to achieve total immersion and connection with text. The same can be said for writing. Building writing stamina, the volume we write, and our commitment to developing our craft is essential. Students need to understand that writing begets writing: the more you write, the better writer you will be. So provide opportunities for students to develop their writing muscles. They need time to generate ideas, focus their attention on a topic, be engrossed in drafting a piece, play with words and craft, and get caught up in text creation. In the words of Regie Routman, "Stamina calls for sufficient know-how, determination, staying power, and resilience" (2012, pg. 147). All are attributes of proficient and passionate writers.

Through daily writing opportunities at either home or school, students strengthen their writing muscles. They attain greater fluidity in their writing, which leads to an increased level of productivity and a sense of accomplishment. The strategies here will jump start writing, increase volume, and lead to a repertoire of pieces that can be polished and refined for publication.

Quick Writes

Without a doubt, Linda Rief is the official matriarch of quick writes. Over the course of her 40-year teaching career, she has written many professional resources that explore this powerful writing technique:
100 Quickwrites: Fast and Effective Freewriting Exercises That Build Students' Confidence, Develop Their Fluency, and Bring Out the Writer In Every Student, 2003
Inside the Writer's–Reader's Notebook: A Workshop Essential, 2007
The Quickwrite Handbook: 100 Mentor Texts to Jumpstart Your Students' Thinking and Writing, 2018

According to Linda Rief, "A *quickwrite* is a first draft response to a short piece of writing, usually no more than one page of poetry or prose, a drawing, an excerpt from a novel or a short picture book… This is writing to find writing, but using someone else's words to stimulate their thinking." (2018, pg. 3)

The structure of a quickwrite is simple: post the model/mentor text for all to see; read it aloud so students can hear it; and ask students to do a quick write in response, based on a few open-ended prompts. Students are asked to write for just a few minutes. Once writers have finished drafting, invite willing participants to share.

We have found that when we provide students with a model/mentor and an opportunity to respond freely, they are more likely to accept the invitation to write and commit to the task at hand. Some of the benefits of quick writing:
- Provides students with ideas and stimulus to write from
- Facilitates occasions for students see stylistic devices and craft techniques in action from quality mentor texts
- Affords writing opportunities that are invitational, short, low-risk
- Helps students create a bank of writing from which they can pull to develop more elaborate pieces
- Enables consciousness to flow uncensored, due to the speed of the activity
- Offers regular opportunities for writing practice in a meaningful, purposeful, and personal way
- Honors student ownership and choice over what they write
- Delivers surprises and *aha!* moments for writers and builds their confidence

Selecting model/mentor texts for quickwrites is a mindful process. They are carefully chosen to reflect a specific purpose and are provocative in nature: format, craft techniques, style, organization, literacy devices, feelings, etc.

The gift of quick writing is that it does not enable the writer to overthink, censor, or edit. Students are able to draft with a measure of support that honors their voice and creativity.

Prompt Power

Prompt-based writing has been around and successful forever, due to its simplicity, ease of use, and the advantages it offers writers. Prompts are an invitation to a focused topic and often propose a particular feeling, situation, or idea. They teach the writer to observe closely, think deeply, and feel authentically. The short statements stimulate interest in a novel idea, enable writers to try something new, help get ideas flowing, and narrow the decision for those who are overwhelmed by unlimited choice. Prompts are very similar to quick writes but with one major difference: a prompt is very directed, whereas a quick write is vastly open-ended.

Select prompts that will be meaningful and compelling to your writers and connect to area of writing focus. For example, *The Mysteries of Harris Burdick* by Chris Van Allsburg is a wonderful resource for stimulating narrative writing. Some other texts we would recommend to support prompt-based writing:

Aimee Chase, *One Question a Day for Kids*

Teresa Klepinger, *Cliffhanger Writing Prompts: 30 One-page Story Starters*

Emily Winfield Martin, *The Imaginaries: Little Scraps of Larger Stories*

Jay Sacher, *The Amazing Story Generator: Creates Thousands of Writing Prompts*

John Burningham, *Would You Rather...*

> There are many websites that offer free writing prompts, including:
> https://thinkwritten.com/writing-prompts-for-kids/
> https://www.journalbuddies.com
> https://conversationstartersworld.com/would-you-rather-questions-for-kids/

Free Writing

In his book *Joy Write*, Ralph Fletcher espouses writing that is "...low-stakes, informal, student-centered" (2017, pg. xii). He points out that this type of writing is ideal for helping students to

- find their stride as writers
- experience the joy, pleasure, and passion of writing
- define/identify themselves as writers

Opportunities to write, free from teacher direction, a prompt, a mentor text, or assessment, is liberating. It is writing that allows students to be in the driver's seat and travel down any road they choose. *Invigorating*, *refreshing*, and *energizing* are just some of the words our students have used to describe these wild and wonderful writing times, when they get to choose, free from teacher interference. So hands off, step back, and let the writing flow!

Writing to Become More Appreciative Readers

The Louvre in Paris, the Museum of Modern Art in New York City, the Royal Ontario Museum in Toronto, the National Gallery in London, and Accademia Gallery in Florence—these renowned galleries are treasure troves of rich cultural and historical artifacts. If you have ever had the privilege of visiting one of these museums, chances are you have been offered either a guided tour or an audio device to enhance your experience. We highly recommend that you take advantage of these informative methods of commentary, as they significantly enrich your experience. For example, when you are viewing a piece of art, the guide provides valuable information about the painter, the time period, the imagery, and the skill and technique used, as well as the hidden symbols and messages the average viewer would be unaware of.

Our writers need a guide when they are interacting with and exploring text. Draw their attention to the organization, structure, craft techniques, stylistic elements, word choice, imagery, sentence fluency, and general sound of the text to their reader's ear. Help them notice the moves the author makes to engage the reader and enhance the reading experience. When we learn to notice, note, and appreciate the artistry of the author, it heightens our reading experience. As writers, we are inspired and learn from mentor authors. We savor, relish, and delight in what we read and are compelled to mirror their craft and style.

In order to immerse our writers in an authentic reading experience, the first read must be for pure enjoyment and appreciation. Subsequent readings are purposefully intended for reading like a writer, with ears and eyes open. The work of the following authors are places to start looking:

Diana Hutts Aston & Sylvia Long	Lester Laminack
David Bouchard	Patricia Polacco
Eve Bunting	Cynthia Rylant
Nicola Davies	Seymour Simon
The Fan Brothers	Chris Van Allsburg
Ralph Fletcher	Jane Yolen
Elin Kelsey	

Once you start looking, the options will exceed your reading time! And your student writing will reap the benefits from their writing author mentors.

Writing to Share Valuable Life Lessons

Stories we read have the capacity to teach each of us about stewardship, belonging, kindness, acceptance, honesty, empathy, and compassion, among other important lessons. Their power to share, illustrate, and impart life lessons is immense. Our students often see their lives reflected in text and exclaim, "Me too! Something just like that has happened to me." As writing teachers, we snatch up those opportune moments and encourage our writers to pick up their pen and tell their story, because their life, their experiences, their adventures, their challenges and missteps are lessons for others to learn from.

In *I Didn't Stand Up* by Lucy Falcone, a young bystander does not stand up for the innocent victims being targeted around him. When he becomes the target, he wonders who will stand up for him. We all can identify a time in our life when we turned a blind eye to unkind, disrespectful actions and merely walked away. Write about it. In *The Most Magnificent Thing* by Ashley Spires, a young girl desires to create a magnificent creation but becomes frustrated and angry, and abruptly quits. Her dog encourages her to persevere and she learns that, with time and effort, she is able to achieve her goal. When have you been overwhelmed, threw up your hands, and wanted to quit, but instead chose to recommit, change your mindset, and get the job done? Write about it. In *One Green Apple* by Eve Bunting, newcomer Farrah faces challenges and struggles on her first day of school visiting the apple orchard. Every one of us has experienced being an outsider and felt uncomfortable and unsure. The kindness of a stranger has made a world of difference. Write about it. Books are powerful stimuli for our writing lives.

Writing ideas that contain life lessons most often come from real life. Draw your students' attention to crucial moments written on their heart and branded into their memories. This week alone, Anne directed writers to record the following ideas in their notebooks:

> Ethan stole a Rubik's cube from another student's cubbie and was caught on camera. His parents decided the consequence was that Ethan was to select a recent Christmas toy to donate to Goodwill so he would experience and hopefully understand what it feels like to lose something you love. Write about it!

> Josie made a rude and hurtful video about a former friend and posted it on her social media account. Of course, her ex-friend discovered the video, but so did Josie's family and the school principal. Having her family, the principal, and the school police officer talk to her about the consequences and implications of her actions was intense for Josie. Their hope is that Josie has learned the impact of her reckless act on others and herself. Write about it!

Mohammad and his classmates recently read an article in the local newspaper that spoke of the challenges some citizens were having navigating the snow-covered sidewalks in their community. With the support of their teacher, they wrote letters to their local councillor and even brought in snow shovels to tackle the sidewalks until a more permanent solution could be found. This is a lesson in kindness, using your voice, and community engagement. Write about it!

Each of these examples illustrates how everyday events, positive and negative, can be channelled into writing that teaches others a life lesson.

Writing to Describe, Explain, Entertain, and Persuade

One of the most important reasons that we, as human beings, choose to write is very simple: to communicate. Whether writing is public or private, we are intentionally putting our voice onto a page for a purpose. As in science, where the taxonomy of living things allows us to organize and understand species, reading genres and writing forms are helpful categorization systems. At some point in time, wise individuals created a classification system to help us navigate the world of literacy. For example, just consider the number of genres that we read: realistic fiction, mystery, historical fiction, thrillers, science fiction, fantasy, non-fiction, biography/autobiography, etc. Once readers are knowledgeable about genre, they develop preferences, an awareness of how text is structured, and specific features to be found within. The categories that writing is most often divided into are purpose-driven: to Describe, to Explain, to Entertain, and to Persuade, or DEEP.

See page 56 for more on writing formats.

During free writing, merely posing the question "Why are you writing this piece?" is a powerful conversation starter. It calls on writers to consider DEEP—the purpose of their composition—and compels them to reflect on their personal writing reasons. Most often the driver for free writing is the idea rather than the form/purpose. Teacher-led writing, on the other hand, is most often driven by purpose. We select the form and invest instructional time teaching the specific structure, techniques, and features of that form. Once students have grasped these elements, they are able to make informed decisions about which format would best suit their message and audience. Whether the writing is student- or teacher-driven, the question *Why write?* must be answered!

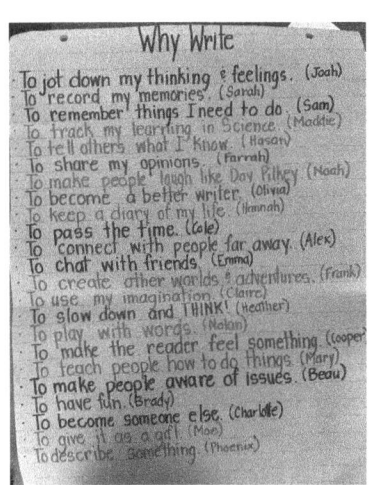

> ### *Ask Your Students*
>
> We want our students to recognize that the gift of writing is its own reward. The activities described throughout this chapter show your students the many benefits of writing. Now it's time to ask your students to answer the vital question: *Why write?* Be prepared to be mesmerized by the countless reasons they identify. Be sure to collect their thinking on a Why Write anchor chart and prominently display it in the classroom for all to see! As more writing reasons are discovered, add them to the chart.

My Triple-C Card

curious...capable...confident

Name: _____

- _____
- _____
- _____
- _____
- _____
- _____
- _____
- _____
- _____
- _____
- _____
- _____
- _____
- _____
- _____
- _____

6

Fifth Step: Provide What Students Need to Write

HGTV has nothing on teachers! We are constantly remodeling and reorganizing. Despite the fact that we cannot renovate our classrooms by taking down walls, installing more cupboards, or even adding our own personal bathroom, we too have issues with and complaints about our spaces. We end up taking on the role of interior designer and attempt to create an environment that meets our needs and requirements.

As teachers, we must take into account what we want to do in our writing classrooms. Our priorities are

- a large gathering area that will seat the entire class
- a small-group meeting area for conferences and focused instruction
- various nooks around the room where students can curl up and write
- a space for a diverse and abundant classroom library filled with mentor texts
- multiple spaces for published work to be displayed

And don't forget the attractive décor—plants, cushions, and lamps.

We want visitors to our classroom, adult or student, to know that this environment is home to a writing community. Does the physical design and layout of your space clearly communicate that this is a room where writers live? We know what you're thinking: Have you seen the size of my room? Do you know how many students I have? Do you know how big the desks are? We all face those challenges when arranging our classrooms. But we have to be creative and work with what we've got. Building the physical space for our writing community takes intention and creativity. So let's investigate the rationale for each element.

Writing by the Numbers

Gathering the Class

Have you ever been out for dinner with friends and had the whole group spread out down a long rectangular table? You may have been eagerly anticipating the enjoyment of catching up, visiting, and chatting with particular peeps you haven't

Think for a moment of sports teams: the home of the Toronto Raptors is the Air Canada Centre, the Montreal Canadians live at the Bell Centre, the New York Yankees reside at Yankee Stadium, and the Green Bay Packers inhabit Lambeau Field. Every team, squad, or club has a space that unites and bonds them. The large gathering area in your room becomes the home of your writing community. The ritual of coming together in this defined space is symbolic.

seen in a while, only to realize that you are confined to conversing with those who are directly across from and beside you. When this happens to us, we enjoy the conversations we are a part of, but also find ourselves curious about other conversations and the laughter at the end of the table, and what we may have missed out on—FOMO, indeed.

When our students are seated around the room and are asked to interact with a neighbor, they are limited to conversing with those who are in close proximity to them, and sometimes this is suitable and sufficient. Other times, when our intention is to engage, share, and discuss as a writing community, desks and tables are no longer the place to be! It is time to draw the gang together in a large gathering area, preferably carpeted for comfort. Having a close communal area is a non-negotiable for us, as it is the location that unifies and cements us as a community of writers. When you are reading mentor text and sharing writing, having your students physically gathered close as one group is vital because proximity matters.

Proximity to the Text

We want our students to actively engage and interact with what we are reading to and with them. For example, when we are reading a picture book as a mentor text for writing, we want them close, so we can draw their attention to a line or craft technique found in text. Likewise, during quick writes, whether using a big book or a projection on a screen or the interactive whiteboard, students must be able to clearly read the passage. Focusing their eyes and ears on the page increases their investment and engagement with the written mentor.

Proximity to the Teacher

> #### *Anne*
>
> Last March break, I went with my family to New York City and took in the play *My Fair Lady* at Lincoln Center. What made it an extraordinary experience was the fact that we were merely five rows from centre stage. The seats were worth every penny. Being that close to the stage let us clearly see every nuance and emotion on the actors' faces.

Luckily our students get to have front-row seats to us every time we draft and compose text—at no charge! We want to be able to look right into their eyes, to hook their minds and touch their hearts. This requires that they be in close proximity to the lead writer in the class composing the text in front of them, not sitting back in recesses of the room.

Proximity to One Another

The large gathering area serves to nourish and support your steadily growing writing community and your interconnectedness with one another.

The authentic conversation that occurs during teacher-modeled writing, drafting co-constructed text, and sharing completed compositions benefits from proximity as well. The ability to express our thoughts and perspectives and to build on the thinking of one another is supported by physical closeness. It also increases student engagement in the conversation and facilitates dialogue within the community. This can lead to the creation of shared understandings about craft techniques, stylistic elements, word choice, etc.

Small Groups Unite

Just as there is power in the entire classroom writing community coming together to interact with mentor text, to observe modeled writing, and to engage in interactive writing and sharing of compositions, the case can be made for having a space in our classrooms for small groups to congregate. Whether you gather on the floor on comfortable pillows, cluster chairs around a small table, or sit in a guided-reading horseshoe, the fact is that you need a space to be eye-to-eye, to lean in, and to chat with one another about your writing. The purpose of a small-group meeting area is to provide an intimate location away from the bustle of the class to meet for focused instruction, writing conferences, and private sharing. Spaces for small groups to collaborate and communicate are essential to a writing community.

A Nook for One

As mentioned in Chapter 4, deciding where to write is a personal choice authors make. We must be sensitive to the fact that some of our writers require spaces that are quiet, calm, and cozy to compose. They find a bustling, humming environment distracting, disruptive, and even frustrating to work in. We have found in conversation that most of our developing writers require comfort and quiet to immerse themselves in their ideas and writing. So if we are committed to providing precious time for students to engage themselves in writing, why would we not provide them with an optimal environment?

Where are the comfy, cozy, quiet places in your room for students to curl up and draft? When arranging classroom furniture, mindfully create little nooks around the room where students can get comfortable and be alone with a notebook or clipboard. We want them to be able to write like they naturally do outside of school; many identify their bedroom as that space. With this in mind, try to offer homey, relaxed, intimate spaces. So hit shops, thrift stores, and garden centres in search of comfortable chairs, coffee tables, rugs, and décor. Summer is the perfect time to purchase affordable, kid-friendly furniture. We have had great luck with outdoor lawn chairs in a variety of colors, sizes, and designs. Consider plastic Muskoka chairs, beach chairs, beanbags, oversized pillows, and carpet squares. These attractive writing areas offer an alternative to the formal chair and desk. They add to the writing atmosphere in the room and replicate authentic writing places outside the classroom.

Tools of the Trade

If you love to travel, you probably have a drawer or bin filled with special items you have purchased specifically to carry on a flight: hand sanitizer, eye-glass cleaner, emery board, nuts, hand wipes, water, gum, Tylenol, eye mask, tissues, granola bar, band-aids, vitamins, a book. What we choose to pack in our carry-on is personal and subjective. It stems from our needs, likes, and past experiences.

What to Write With

Developing writers are often unaware and not acquainted with the wealth of writing instruments and tools they can use to write with. This shouldn't surprise us, given that typically students are given an HB pencil and a photocopied template or workbook to write in. Don't get us wrong—sometimes it is necessary to select the tool and products students will use. We do this for ease, according to resource availability, and to set students up for drafting success and writing purpose. But it's important to remember that adult writers have very specific preferences for what we write with and what we write on. Mary uses a fine-point Zebra refillable pen to take notes in a lined journal, while she prefers a 0.5 mechanical pencil when drafting in her writer's notebook, and Staedtler fine-liner markers to draw and doodle with. Anne rarely if ever drafts in anything but a pencil, but when taking notes for work she must have a Dixon porous, fine-point Trend pen. She detests notebooks without lines and uses fine-point Sharpies to draw and sketch with. What are your tools of the trade? What must you have in your pencil case to draft with? What are your paper preferences?

If we want to support our developing writers in finding devices they are comfortable using, put them at ease, and are aesthetically pleasing to them, we must provide them time to play, explore, and experiment with a variety of tools to find what works for them and fits comfortably in their hand. Consider setting up a writing-tool station in your classroom that is stocked with various writing instruments:

- pencils: standard and mechanical
- ink pens of various colors
- porous pens of various colours
- markers: fine-tipped and medium point
- pencil crayons
- highlighters
- erasers

As a writing teacher, you are somewhere on the continuum of control: you may be a free spirit who allows students to self-select their tools, or someone who more often maintains control by determining what students use and when. We believe that the best place to be is somewhere in the middle, allowing students time to discover and uncover their likes and dislikes while providing opportunities for them to experience different possibilities. This enables them to develop their own writing identity and personality. You can determine and select when it is suitable and applicable to play with different tools.

What to Write On

> *Anne*
>
> I fondly remember trips to mall with my tween girlfriends to wander around the shops, hit up the food court, and maybe make a purchase or two with babysitting money. One store in particular was a required destination—Whimsy. A favourite area of the store was the stationery section, which was jam-packed with individually priced decorative paper and coordinating envelopes. For merely 25 cents per sheet of paper and

> another 35 cents for a matching envelope, I would have beautiful, high-quality paper on which to write letters to family and friends. Stationery was chosen with the recipient in mind: horses galloping in a field for my cousin Angie, sprays of flowers spreading across the page for my Aunt Jean, an ocean lighthouse scene for my Nanny. The purpose of the paper was to write a letter and the quality of the paper was special, just like person receiving it.

Other items you may consider adding to your writing station:
- clipboards
- dictionaries and thesauruses
- high-frequency word lists
- folders
- writing checklists
- anchor charts
- writing format success criteria
- pre-made books
- prompt cards
- idea jar

Offering different paper products to students for them to write on adds a sense of delight and excitement to the task. Colored, lined, dense, decorative, parchment, blank, cards, notepads, scrap paper, sticky notes—the choices are numerous and novel. But students must learn how to make paper choices based on their writing purpose. GOOS (Good On One Side) paper is perfect to jot, scribble, note, squiggle, doodle, sketch, record, list, etc., whereas decorative, dense paper is suited to presentation writing, gift writing, letter writing. So add an assortment of stationery to your writing station to support your writers in their work. Just remember to teach students to not be wasteful and to select carefully based on writing purpose.

Stowing Students' Stashes

Crumpled, wrinkled, ripped, creased, tattered and torn—something strange occurs when a child places a piece of paper within the confines of their desk. We imagine a little paper pixie anxiously awaiting the arrival of more paper to ravage and destroy. When we ask students to locate a draft, what they remove from their desk resembles something from the recycling bin. Or they waste precious writing time just trying to find their paper! This is exceptionally frustrating for us as teachers, especially when we believe we have created the ideal conditions for students to engage in writing. We have provided the time, space, and materials but, once students begin to draft and publish their pieces, the question emerges: Where are they going to stow their stash in an organized fashion?

The answer comes down to personal preference, cost, and space. We have seen everything from a writing folder, a binder, a two-pocket organizer, and an individual file folder system. Subdivided folders provide a built in sorting system: drafts on one side, published pieces on the other. These options can easily be stored in desks, bins, or cubbies because they are relatively flat and thin. Other options teachers have shared with us are storage drawers for student tables, plastic bins with hanging files, and paper tray cubby units. Depending on the space available in your classroom, determine the place to store your students' writing in an organized manner.

The Classroom Library

A house painter needs dropcloths, tape, brushes, rollers, stir sticks—and, don't forget, paint. A makeup artist needs brushes, sponges, swabs, false eye lashes, hair clips, cleaning wipes—and, don't forget, makeup. A potter needs a wheel, an apron, needles, wires, sponges, water, a kiln—and, don't forget, clay. A writer needs paper, writing instruments, a Writer's Notebook, a dictionary/thesaurus for editing—and, don't forget, books! You can't cultivate a writing life without books! Every profession has tools, and writers need books! Lots and lots of books and magazines are the currency on which our writing community grows, thrives, and flourishes. Literacy guru Regie Routman states

> The most critical piece for teaching writing well is the "right" text. Almost every well-known author credits being an avid reader as being the most significant factor in becoming a writer. (Routman, 2012, p. 61)

As the curator of the classroom environment, you must bring in the books: books to read, savor, dissect, mimic, springboard off, piggyback on, imitate, emulate. A classroom library is an essential element of every literacy environment. You might be thinking: "We have an outstanding school library that we visit every cycle. Why do I need my own library?" The reason is that one library visit every cycle is not enough to cultivate a reading/writing life. You want to create an environment in which students are surrounded by text so that books and mentors are always within reach. A classroom library is never closed; its hours of operation are from the time the first student enters the room until the last student walks out the door. These books are always within our grasp.

It is also more manageable for teachers to know the books in their classroom libraries. Familiarity with your classroom library collection allows you to readily match texts to readers. You're able to quickly respond to students' requests, to suggest alternatives, and to make recommendations. As the lead writer, you can pull specific text to model a format you are exploring, to illustrate a craft technique, and to emphasis a particular stylistic device. Knowing your collection well allows you to identify what is there, what is not there, and what gaps exist between your collection and students' needs and interests as readers and writers.

Our classroom libraries are carefully customized to match the age, maturity, reading ability, and interests of our students. We enhance the collection with text tied to curriculum writing expectations, keeping in mind specific text forms/formats, vivid language, word choice, figurative devices, etc. For example, in Ontario Grade 3, students learn how to write a familiar story from a new perspective. Wonderful mentor texts to model the concept with include

- Lisa Campbell Ernst, *The Gingerbread Girl*
- Jeanie Franz Ransom, *What Really Happened to Humpty?*
- Jon Sciezska, *The True Story of the Three Little Pigs*
- Capstone Publishers' The Other Side of the Story: a series of 18 books that tell fairy tales from a new perspective, with subtitles like *The Story of Cinderella as told by the Wicked Stepmother, The Story of Little Red Riding Hood as Told by the Wolf, The Story of the Three Bears as Told by Baby Bear, The Story of the Three Billy Goats Gruff as Told by the Troll, The Story of Rapunzel told by Dame Gothel*, etc.

Other must-have authors and titles, filled to the brim with vivid language, stunning word choice, and fantastic figurative devices are

Please note this is by no means an exhaustive list, just a few of our favorite titles and go-to authors!

- David Bouchard, *The Elders are Watching*
- Julie Brinckloe, *Fireflies*
- Nicola Davies, *The Promise*
- Ralph Fletcher, *Twilight Comes Twice*
- John Frank, *The Toughest Cowboy or How the Wild West Was Tamed*
- Elizabeth Friedrich, *Leah's Pony*

Dianna Hutts Aston and Sylvia Long, *A Rock is Lively*
Elin Kelsey, *You Are Stardust*
Lester Laminack, *Saturdays and Teacakes*
Lester Laminack, *The King of Bees*
George Ella Lyon, *Book*
Kate Messener, *Up in the Garden and Down in the Dirt*
Libba Moore Gray, *My Mama Had a Dancing Heart*
Pam Muñoz Ryan, *Hello Ocean*
Kenard Pak, *Goodbye Autumn, Hello Winter*
Jean E. Pendziwol, *Me and You and the Red Canoe*
Hanoch Piven, *My Dog is As Smelly As Dirty Socks: and Other Funny Family Portraits*
Hanock Piven, *My Best Friend is As Sharp As a Pencil: and Other Funny Classroom Portraits*
Patricia Polacco, *When Lightening Comes in a Jar*
Cynthia Rylant, *Snow*
Cynthia Rylant, *Life*
Charles R. Smith, *Rimshots: BASKETBaLL PiX, RoLLs, and RhyTHms*
Chris Van Allsburg, *Just a Dream*
Megan Wagner Lloyd, *Finding Wild*
Jacqueline Woodson, *Show Way*
Jane Yolen, *Owl Moon*
Jane Yolen, *The Scarecrow's Dance*

In our classroom we have complete control over which books are displayed and featured. We can choose which authors, series, genres, forms/formats, and even text sets to spotlight in a variety of creative ways. Your classroom library is well-read by you, the writing teacher. We cannot stress enough the power, influence, and ability you hold as the lead writer in the room when you can speak authentically about the texts that are a part of your collection and quickly put into hands of your students the text they need. It is imperative that we, as writing teachers, read as many of the books in our collection as possible. This allows us to genuinely book talk titles, to reliably link specific writers with books that will be serve as quality mentors, and to have sincere writing conversations with students. Together these actions cultivate the will to write well in our students.

Despite the fact that we are self-proclaimed book addicts and have the overflowing book shelves and stacks on the floor to prove it, a handful of good-quality mentor texts is really all you need. Returning to a core set of texts again and again has many benefits to readers and listeners. Comprehension can take a back seat and be replaced with a focus on the authors' use of language, craft, and style. Listeners are encouraged to stop the reader and note beautiful lines and phrases, places where the author's artistry comes through. When we take time to pick, mine, and snatch examples of onomatopoeia, simile, alliteration, magic of three, noun-verb pairing, etc., we empower our student writers to play and develop their own skills as authors.

In particular we encourage you to create a special bin for your mentor texts and flag the cover with a sticky note, identifying unique craft techniques and stylistic devices featured in the text. Mary has been doing this for years with her books and attests to its power in reinforcing the use of mentor texts. When these books are collected together in an easily accessible location, students are more apt to use them as a valuable resource when writing. Having the craft techniques found within notes helps students quickly locate the text that will serve as a mentor for a specific technique. For example, in *My Mama Had a Dancing Heart*, Libba Moore Gray expertly employs noun-verb pairings: *leaf-kicking, leg-lifting, hand-clapping*. In *Quick as a Cricket*, Audrey Wood skilfully uses similes: *sad as a basset, slow as a snail, small as an ant, wild as a chimp*. Mentor texts become teachers. There is no escaping the value of a classroom library to our developing writers.

Appraising Your Classroom Library

In our system, school librarians are required to critically inspect their collection each year. Similarly, we need to scrutinize our classroom libraries annually. Use the following questions as a guide:

- Would you categorize your library as current and fresh or dated and tired?
- Would you say your library is abundant? Solid? Or limited? Do you believe your students have plenty of choice?
- Does your library contain various genres, forms, and formats? Fiction: realistic, historical, fantasy, mystery, adventure, humor? Nonfiction: biography, autobiography, memoir, earth and space, people and places, animals? Formats: articles, report, letters, fables, legends, myths, recounts, procedures, reviews, op.eds, instructions, etc.? What about poetry?
- Can students access tried-and-true authors and shiny and new titles/mentors in your library?
- Will students be able to easily locate favorite authors/mentors in the library?
- Does your library accommodate a range of reading abilities?
- Will students find lighter gateway (i.e., quick-read, hi-lo) text in the collection, books that provide them an entry point into reading as they develop their stamina and love of well-written literature?
- Will students discover books that honor a writing life and the writing process; for example, *A Writer's Notebook: Unlocking the Writer Within You* by Ralph Fletcher; *Writing Radar: Using Your Journal to Snoop Out and Craft Great Stories* by Jack Gantos; *Nothing Ever Happens on 90th Street* by Roni Schotter?
- Is your library inclusive? Does it promote a sense of belonging? Will your students see themselves and their life stories reflected in the texts found in your library? Does it honor the diversity of your classroom, larger community, and greater world?
- Will your classroom library support students in gaining background knowledge related to topics they wish to write about?
- Do you routinely add to the collection throughout the school year as interests and preferences emerge and change? As students grow as writers, do you change the books?

Picky and Particular

For many of us, our favorite stores are our local book stores. We can be found on the floor of our local Chapters, browsing books, perusing pages, and mining for mentors. Building a precise and particular library collection takes time and money. We suggest new teachers, or teachers new to a division, consider the following ideas for growing your library:

- In our city, we are lucky to have a number of used book stores as well as donation centres that focus on gently used books. Their great selection and affordable prices make it feasible to come away with a stack. However, we strongly suggest being a critical consumer. Select books that are appealing to the eye—stay away from yellow, tattered, or worn books. If they look dated and dirty, students will not pick them up. Let's face it, neither would you. Select books that are appealing to the ear—ones that clamor to be read aloud, compel us to stop and savor, demand to be reread with relish, and long to be emulated in our writing.

- Scholastic book clubs are a phenomenal source for current and affordable titles. Their bonus points program enables you to take advantage of student sales and use the points earned to augment your collection. Each month, be sure to peruse the flyer with your writing program in mind.
- It is not the classroom teacher's sole responsibility to finance the classroom library. Use the power of persuasion (and the information in this book) to make a pitch to your administrator and Home and School Association to financially support your growing classroom library. It takes a whole school community to cultivate a writer, and each stakeholder must contribute.

In Chapter 3, we examined the valuable information gathered from student interest and writing surveys. These sources provide you with students' particular writing preferences and sources for idea generation, as well as insight into the kinds of writing students do at home and school, and the craft techniques they use most often in their writing. It's key that students see their interests reflected in the classroom library, since it serves as a source of background knowledge and a stimulus for ideas, and is the ultimate source for writing mentors. Use this information to guide your selections for the class. For example if students are passionate about outer space or endangered species, are investigating writing biographies or intentionally playing with onomatopoeia, then make sure your library contains books that honor such curiosities and interests.

Include Nonfiction

While attending a recent literacy conference in Toronto, we were awestruck by the spectacular nonfiction reading material for sale. Displays featured the following topics: mountain gorillas, lacrosse, the NBA, tornadoes, global warming, baking, crafts, science experiments, and Ancient Egypt. Ensuring that our classroom libraries contain nonfiction is imperative.

- Children are naturally curious and want to know more about our world. Nonfiction is the door to endless information. While capitalizing on students' personal interests, it also serves to build their background knowledge and provides inspiration for writing topics.
- Gone are the days of getting facts and information from a 20-volume encyclopaedia or heavily bound textbooks that students were not permitted to take home. *Dusty, smelly,* and *yellowed* are just some of the words used to describe these tomes. In recent years, we have been blessed with the emergence of new genres, such as informational fiction and narrative nonfiction. These genres offer readers factual information in a familiar style and format that increases engagement and aids in comprehension. The various literacy techniques utilized by authors make it beautiful to the ear, appealing to the readers senses.
- At one time nonfiction text was quite expensive to purchase and often written at levels inaccessible for growing readers. Not so anymore! An eruption of stunning, engaging, readable texts has emerged. The layouts, colors, and fonts appeal to students' aesthetic while at the same time broadening student

knowledge. Writers are eager to replicate two-page spreads and layouts found in these captivating texts and are also keen to make use of these features in their own compositions.
- The majority of what we read and write as adults is nonfiction. Providing our students with opportunities to frequently interact with nonfiction text prepares them for this future.
- Nonfiction topics and titles support our curriculum, especially in science and social studies. Guaranteeing that our classroom libraries contain texts that connect with our curriculum extends the learning for our students. Merging content areas and language expectations provides authentic writing opportunities for students.

Documenting the Writing Journey with Writing Records

Recording the events of our lives is a practice as old as time. Births, deaths, weddings, weather, tragedies, political events—you name it, it has been documented by our ancestors. Our past can be found scribbled in family Bibles, hidden in musty diaries, displayed in photo albums and scrapbooks. These primary sources are windows into our past and inform our future.

Encourage growing writers to formally document and reflect on the writing they publish in a brief record. This tool becomes evidence of where students have ventured on their writing journey over the course of a school year: the topics they have been driven to explore, the forms/formats they most frequently write, and what they have learned about themselves as a writer. Above all, writing records are a tool to cultivate writers. They nourish our writing community. Because the writing record is completed when students publish a piece, it serves as a reflection tool at writing conferences between teacher and student; they are not viewed as busy work. Students know and understand their purpose and value them as a writing tool. All it takes is a simple, quick recording of the date, identification as free writing or assigned writing, form/format, topic, and what they learned about themselves as writers; see page 116 for the My Writing Publication Record template. The writing record should be neither tedious nor time-consuming to complete.

> Since a writing record is a yearlong compilation of a student's work, it provides the student with an overview of their writing journey. It illustrates their growth and change over time. They remember, reminisce, and revisit previous pieces, stories, and places they have taken readers.

Tracing Writing Territories

If our aim is to ensure that each student explores various forms/formats and topics, how do we determine if they are meeting this goal? Reviewing writing records with students during conferences allows us to celebrate the formats students are writing and topics they enjoy focusing on. While, as teachers, we are clearly aware of what formats we assign to students for writing, it is worthwhile to know what formats and topics they gravitate toward when given opportunities for free writing.

Conversation-Starter for Conferences and Goal-Setting

Conferences can begin with a review of a student writing record. They are windows into the writing lives of our students. They provide us with a number of pieces of information, such as

- what students have completed/published
- the amount of free writing students are engaging in
- what formats they are choosing to write
- the topics they are drawn to
- what they have learned about themselves as a writer

Conversations about what students have learned about themselves as writers enable us to authentically co-construct a writing goal that is tailored to each writer's growth and development.

Acknowledgment and Celebration

When reflecting on a writing record over a term or a year, students experience a sense of pride and accomplishment. They can easily lose sight of the texts they have written when they are not documented. The writing record is a testament to what they have written, formats they have explored, topics they have entertained, and the craft techniques and literacy devices with which they have experimented.

The Four P's: Publication, Permission, Presentation, Plagiarism

Publication

In his video *Improving Adolescent Writers*, renowned literacy leader Kelly Gallagher states that "Writing is never done—it is just due" (2008). At some point, students must put down the pen and submit/share their writing with an audience, typically their teacher. Regularly publishing pieces shows that students have generated an idea, sometimes selected the format, produced an initial draft, revised the piece for clarity and craft, and edited for conventions. They cannot live in a world of incomplete drafts and unfinished pieces; they must invest time and energy into improving, enhancing, and refining their work, and then clean up their pieces by editing for spelling and grammar. The final step is publishing and releasing the work to an audience. Taking a piece to publication is a part of the process.

Permission

When we create the conditions for students to write freely from a place of authenticity and lived experience, we must tackle the issue of permission. By creating spaces where students feel safe, are willing to be vulnerable, and expose their intimate thoughts and feelings, we have the responsibility and obligation to honor their privacy and wishes. If students are expected or decide to publish a piece, we believe they have a right to determine the audience beyond us. Seeking consent prior to displaying work honors the writers in the room, empowers them to know they are the keepers of their stories and voice, and sends the clear message that they are the owners of their writing.

> *Anne*
>
> When I assigned memoir writing, I realized that a few students chose to write about highly emotional and sensitive events in their lives, such as the recent loss of a beloved aunt, the separation of their parents, the trauma of being in a refugee camp. Out of consideration for their openness, I sought permission before publicly posting their work on a bulletin board.

Presentation

For many artists, the hours of effort and energy dedicated to their art culminates in a celebratory performance. In the same way, our writers need opportunities to publicly present their work to an audience beyond the teacher. Published authors write for an audience—to entertain, to move, to inspire, and to excite readers. Be sure to provide spaces within the school for students to showcase their work; bulletin boards, hallway displays, library exhibitions, and office windows are the perfect spots to catch a reader.

Public libraries, local businesses, and community centres are other locations to publicly share student writing. For example, Mary once worked with a teacher whose students proudly displayed their descriptive pizza paragraphs in a local pizza parlor; Anne once supported a class in getting their travel brochures exhibited in a community travel agency. Providing students with spaces and places to present their work honors the time and effort they have put into the task. Facilitating opportunities for recognition and celebration fuels them as writers!

Mary would often frame student writing and place it strategically around the school, and she fondly remembers having a designated shelf in the Springfield school library for students to promote their published books.

Plagiarism

A painting bears the artist's signature; a piece of pottery is inscribed with the potter's name or mark; a piece of music is credited to the composer, arranger, and lyricist. Creation means ownership. When we share a piece of text with students, we must consistently and deliberately honor the work of the author by calling attention to their name. While we long for our students to be inspired by the writing of others and use it as a mentor text, we must ensure that they do not copy the work of fellow authors directly. Students must know that they cannot take credit for writing that they haven't done.

My Writing Publication Record

Name: _____

Date	Title/Topic	Free Write or Assigned	Form/Format	What I Learned about Myself as a Writer

7

Sixth Step: Nourish the Will to Write

By embracing the essential steps outlined in the preceding chapters, you've set the groundwork for creating a classroom of wilful writers. This took time, effort, and energy on your part. However, we know that just because you plant a sapling does not mean it will grow and bloom. You must plant it in an ideal location where it will have ample sun, adequate drainage, and room to flourish, not to mention needing to provide it with water and fertilizer those early weeks to boost its chances of survival and growth. Your students need you to be their horticulturist. Writers will thrive and grow in an environment that continually provides them with the essential elements to cultivate their will to write. It's never a one-and-done. It's not an event or a lesson to check off. Cultivating the will to write in developing writers is something we dedicate and commit time to all year long. Just as we devote time to teach the skills of writing each day, we must embrace the opportunity to nourish the will to write daily. Our sixth step is reviewing the five previous steps for cultivating writers and considering ways you can continue to nourish the will to write in your students over the course of the year.

Develop Your Writing Life

To genuinely inspire and motivate our students to be writers, we must be writers ourselves. Your students benefit from a lead writer who ignites enthusiasm and passion for writing. Your personal writing life will openly enable you to spread the love and joy for writing you hold. Interest and desire are contagious! However, your personal writing life cannot be limited to your latest AQ course post or your classroom newsletter and daily emails. It must encompass writing that is connected and related to the writing you are inviting students in your room to do. Your students are depending on you to be a true and faithful writer: someone who does the work and toils with craft; someone who is knowledgeable about forms, formats, and idea generation; someone who leads a writing life and is willing to share their labors with others. When you've done the work, you know the way.

Putting your attempts, cracks, and drafts in front of your students is critical to showing them the process a writer goes through. This level of transparency allows fellow writers to see first-hand that writing is at times messy, challenging, and imperfect. As Penny Kittle says,

> I wasn't supposed to be a *writer*—just someone trying to write—like them. In fact I was a better model because my hesitations and insecurities were just like theirs. It was such a relief to know I didn't have to be good at it; just trying was enough."
> (Kittle, 2008, p. 6)

Sharing your writing with students and making your work public is part of your role as the lead writer and as a member of the writing community. In a vibrant writing classroom, the teacher must put forth their writing on a regular basis to create the conditions for students to be willing to do the same. These activities will support you and your students in making your writing lives public to each other and the entire school community.

Work in Progress

Providing opportunities for all of us, teachers and students alike, to share our unfinished writing is key to developing a community where feedback, guidance, and support is valued. Our writers need to know that despite the fact that writing seems to be a solitary activity, it doesn't need to be. Fellow writers are within arm's reach; they are ready, willing, and able to support writers in their work. Here are a few quick ways to structure that.

Author's Circle

When students wish to elicit feedback, ideas, or suggestions from different people at once, an Author's Circle may be just the format. This routine provides authors with the opportunity to share their developing work with their classmates who, sitting in a circle, lean in to listen intentionally and attentively in response to a request made by the author prior to the reading. This is not about garnering praise, encouragement, or broad feedback; rather, a specific request from the author guides the sharing. For example, Fatima stated, "I have tried to show not tell how my character is feeling. From this segment, what do you think my character is feeling?" Hassan wondered, "I am playing with two different leads for my opinion piece. Which one hooks you, draws you in more, and why?" These frequent opportunities to gather feedback and advice support our writers in the moment rather than delaying their needs until a formal conference is available or scheduled.

Reaction Reading

Mary once read that it's a common practice for acclaimed children's author Robert Munsch to orally share his stories in development when he goes into schools and attends children's festivals. He wishes to test out his creations to see if he is getting the desired response from his listeners. He notices and notes when and where he gets a reaction from the audience; i.e., the potential reader. Our writers need similar opportunities to test out their drafts so that they can note the effect of their writing on the audience and make appropriate revisions to their work. This feedback is helpful and quick. Most classes have buddies who are the ideal audience for writers, but consider also the school librarian, fellow teachers, and administrators as captive audiences for your students to test out their work.

Stuck in the Mud

When the class is in the throes of writing, we all have witnessed a few who appear frustrated, irritated, and stumped by the task at hand. While it is okay and even beneficial to work through challenges and persevere on our own, there are times when we are so stuck that we cannot get out of the mud by ourselves. We need a fellow writer to listen and to offer suggestions and advice to support us in moving past the obstacle. Sometimes that is the lead writer, but we can share the load by encouraging other students to step forward and support their peers. Try stopping writing after 10 minutes and calling out to see if anyone is "stuck in the mud." We sometimes provide students with tiny pylons found at the Dollar Store to place on their desk as a visual calling card if they feel they need assistance, signalling to anyone in the classroom who can offer writing support.

Reading Our Writing Out Loud

The secretaries who sit outside Anne's office, Tammy and Anastasia, often think there is a student or parent in the office due to the sounds slipping out the door, when in fact Anne is often in there alone. When Anne drafts emails, letters, and reports, she always reads her work out loud to hear how it flows and conveys her message. By speaking her writing out loud she is able to hear if her writing makes sense, if it is too formal or casual, and if there are errors and omissions.

The Writing Centre at the University of North Carolina Chapel Hill suggests that there are many benefits to adopting the habit of reading our writing out loud. For example:
- your brain gets information in a new way and you notice things you didn't see before
- you recognize that you might need to reorder sentences or paragraphs or discover that there are gaps in your explanations
- you see that you have moved from one topic to another too abruptly and hear errors in your sentences
- you hear sentences that are awkward, too long, and repetitive
- you hear the tone/impression of the piece and realize it might be too formal or chatty for your intended purpose and audience

(The Writing Centre, 2020)

> Keep in mind that modeling for your students how to slow down the pace of their reading while physically tracking with their finger allows them to effectively hear and identify the blips and bumps in their drafts.

By reading aloud your work, you place yourself in the same position your readers/audience will find themselves. The rhythm and flow of the piece is illuminated when it is read aloud. So support students in developing this beneficial habit by offering them a few ways to engage in this activity.

Private Places: Study carrels, hallways, and quiet corners are just a few of the many secluded locales where writers can read their work free from listening ears.

Whisper Phones: These telephone-esque tools can be purchased from educational suppliers or inexpensively made using PVC pipe from the local hardware store. Students are able to speak quietly into these devices to hear their writing come to life.

Tech Tools: Countless apps and software enable us to record ourselves reading our writing and play it back. Unlike the live reading in the two preceding suggestions, a recording permits us to hit pause and rewind to reflect and revise.

New Releases

Once students have published a piece of writing, it is vital that, if they choose to share their work beyond sharing with the teacher, we provide them with spaces, places, and audiences for their work. In our experience, most students are chomping at the bit to go public with their pieces. They want the praise, applause, and acclaim that comes with a new release. It's a time to celebrate!

Flipping Through the Pages

In Canada, our school year runs for 10 months. Over that time, many pieces of writing will be started, played with, and worked on—but not all will be taken to publication. The pieces that students have chosen or been assigned to take through the entire writing and publishing process have taken considerable work and effort on their part. One way to showcase the growth and development of your writers is to create a bulletin board that features space for each writer to display their published work. Simply create a grid framework that identifies each writer's name and features a photo of them. As each new piece is published, staple it on top of previous work. Viewers are able flip back and read work throughout the year by each author. Consider binding each student's stack of writing into a booklet to celebrate all their published writing throughout the year.

Release Party

As we write this, author and poet Amy Ludwig VanDerwater's highly anticipated new book *Write! Write! Write!* is being released. We have had our order placed for weeks and are eagerly awaiting this new title to arrive. On the author's website, on Twitter and Amazon, this book has been featured and promoted to create a sense of excitement and buzz. We bet she will be holding a special event with family and friends to celebrate and revel in her book's birthday!

Give your students a similar event to spotlight and rejoice in their own publications by holding a release party. Ask each writer to invite a family member as a special guest. To ensure you have enough readers/audience members, reach out to your school community and invite administrators, secretaries, custodians, prep teachers, learning support teachers, etc. Add a sense of style and splendor to the release party by having adequate seating, snacks, soft music, and table decorations. How you structure this event depends on your writers' willingness to share, the space you have, and the number of attendees. For example, each writer can be seated at their desk with their writing in hand and a vacant seat beside them for their guest, with comment cards or sheets on hand so that writers can receive feedback from their readers; attendees travel through the classroom to interact with various authors and comment on their work. Another option is to have keen writers take a seat in the author's chair to read aloud their work for the entire audience; guests are given a pen and stack of comment cards when they arrive to complete as they listen to each piece read aloud. These cards are collected, sorted, and distributed to each author following the event.

A Gift of Writing

Many years ago, Mary was inspired by the concept of gifts of writing as presented by Nancie Atwell in her ground-breaking book *In the Middle*. Describing this as a natural and meaningful reason to write, Nancie tells her students that she writes a poem for her daughter Anne in celebration of her birthday each year:

> I know the bike I give Anne will rust or become too small for her. I understand that the Barbies' heads will fall off and they'll end up at the Boothbay dump. But the things I write for her—my words about her, me, and us—will last forever. These are the best gifts of all for the people we care about." (Atwell, 1998, p. 339)

Pause and Ponder: How will you and your students continue to share your writing and seek feedback throughout the year?

So when its Grandma's birthday, winter celebrations are upon us, or Valentine's Day is around the corner, ask your students to pick up their pens and write. Giving those they love the greatest gift of all benefits both giver and receiver. Student-authors report delighting in the responses they receive from the recipients of their gifts. Mary treasures the comments, notes, and emails she has received from parents whose hearts have been touched by their child's thoughtful and heartfelt words. Writing truly is a gift!

Tap into Your Students' Lives

Writers grow and change over time, so it is vital to frequently check in and monitor the writers in our classrooms. Based on our instruction, the profile of each student will change according to their writing preferences, habits, behaviors, and needs. It's our responsibility to notice, note, and draw attention to the subtle changes, as well as the significant leaps, that writers make in our community. The benefits of knowing your writers abound: it informs your instruction; it fosters the teacher–student writing relationship; it assists you in selecting appropriate mentor text; it enables you to match mentor text to writers; it supports you in connecting writers in your class; it provides valuable data for assessment and evaluation that can be communicated to parents.

Writing Status

We have found that providing opportunities for assigned and free writing on a weekly basis serves different purposes. Assigned writing is linked to curriculum expectations and allows us to model and teach explicitly the features and craft connected to a format in a structured manner. This type of writing is more teacher-led and -driven, and often offers less flexibility. Free writing enables students to exert more ownership, choice, and experimentation with topic, format, and craft. Monitoring the status of your writers on an ongoing basis is important. We attempt to check in with our students each Monday and ascertain what pieces they plan on working on throughout the week during independent writing time. Using a class list or an at-a-glance chart, quickly record information regarding where students are at in the process for each type of writing. Simply checking in with your writing community each week provides the following information:
- where students are at in the writing process (idea generation, drafting, revising, editing, publishing)

- the length of time they are taking to craft a text (e.g., *Chris seems to be writing the never-ending story. Selma seems to be constantly generating ideas but never developing her ideas fully into a piece.*)
- quick patterns and trends in their writing (e.g., *Kathleen's free writing is dominated by poetry which she artfully crafts. Bryce seems to be fixated on hockey as the topic source for all pieces but skilfully weaves his extensive background knowledge into various types of text.*)
- who you need to have a brief chat with
- facts to inform writing conferences

The Writer I Was/The Writer I Am

When beginning a weight-loss and fitness journey, you usually start by establishing your baseline: weight, measurements, BMI, stamina, and strength. This is exactly what we ask students to do when we launch our writing community. They are expected to complete a student writing survey and create an I Am a Writer Who… poem; see page 32. Carefully store these artifacts for the purpose of dusting them off months later for students to use as a reflection tool. Return to each student their previous piece and encourage them to read over and review the information they recorded in the past. Then have students consider how they have grown and changed over time. Adapting Koch's formula "I used to…; Now I…" from *Wishes, Lies, and Dreams: Teaching Children to Write Poetry*, model writing your own writer reflection poem. It is enlightening for students, families, and you to recognize and celebrate each writer's growth. See page 136 for The Writer I Was/The Writer I Am template.

Supplementary Seed Ideas

Being on the lookout for writing ideas and taking time to invest in idea generation is the constant work of a writer. As teachers, we create the conditions for idea stimulation by planning engaging mini-lessons and activities to trigger thoughts, opinions, feelings, and memories. Here are a few extra strategies to support your writing community.

Seasonal Prompts and Special Events: The school calendar overflows with specific events that become memorable moments for student writing: the spirit days many schools host—wacky hair day, twin day, backwards day, jersey day, beach day, etc.; special holidays, such as Halloween, Christmas, Hanukkah, Ramadan, Diwali, Valentine's Day, Easter, Passover, Victoria Day, etc. These events foster creativity, stimulate the imagination, and are just plain fun. So seize these writeable moments!

Goodbyes Are Never Easy: Kristi moved part-way through the year; the class goldfish croaked; Mrs. Beaulac retired at Winter Break; moving out of the house you've grown up in—saying goodbye is filled with emotion and memory. These events can spark emotive and poignant writing. Take time to document these unforgettable eras of our lives.

Times They Are a-Changing: Change is a continual companion in all of our lives. Children rapidly change physically: they grow in height, they lose teeth, they outgrow bikes, they no longer fit into their favorite rubber boots. Environments shift and alter: trees are cut down, pools are installed, vacant lots become strip malls.

Pause and Ponder: How will you purposefully reacquaint yourself with the ever-changing writers in your classroom? How will you continually support writers in accessing, utilizing, and developing their seed ideas?

Relationships ebb and flow: new friends are made, friends become frenemies, parents split, and beloved ones pass away. Reflecting on growth and change is a highly personal and therapeutic exercise. Capture and embrace these notable and sometimes cherished moments in writing.

Model the Habits of a Writer

In Chapter 4 we identified and discussed the habits of a writer who exhibits the will to write. Our emergent authors find their voice through worthwhile idea generation (Finding); they come to know the vast variety of forms and formats they can choose to write in and defining features of each format (Planning); they interact with the community that sustains them through thinking, reading, talking, and sharing (Acting); and they develop goals that will keep them developing their craft (Goal-Setting). All these habits work together to remove writing obstacles and foster the momentum needed to sustain writers. As well, these habits define how we co-construct our writing community, teacher and students together. We set out by intentionally modeling the habits and then coach our students as they come to adopt these routines. Providing students with frequent reminders and opportunities to practice Find, Plan, Act, and Set Goals reinforces and strengthens their commitment and the internalization of these habits. These behaviors support students in becoming lifelong, wilful writers.

The Habit of Finding
Returning, Revisiting, and Revitalizing

> *Anne*
>
> Over the last seven months, I have been on a self-imposed shopping ban. This sanction stemmed from a fall closet clean that brought to glaring light my overabundance of footwear and clothing. As article after article was removed from the closet, I was shocked to discover the immense amount of items I actually had, the things I had forgotten, and the number of pieces that still had tags attached. An intervention was needed. Taking time to evaluate what I had, what fit, what was out of style, what was pilled and faded, and what could be styled into a new outfit helped me sort items into categories of Keep, Toss, and Donate.

Our writer's notebooks can become like Anne's closet. We invest a lot of time generating seed ideas to the point that pages and pages are filled with writing possibilities just waiting to be developed. But often they sit dormant, forgotten, and unused, like so many of Anne's articles of clothing. We must be diligent in modeling and encouraging our writers to return to those precious seeds as sources for writing. Here are a few tangible ways we can support writers in doing just that.

Rereading our Notebooks: Providing specific time for students to reread and revisit a writing mini-lesson explored in their notebook is a meaningful task. Often students have forgotten the precious ideas they had previously planted on the page. Many idea-generation strategies featured in Chapter 3 contain countless ideas for writing. Rereading entries provides opportunities for writers to add to activities and reminds them of ideas they can develop and grow.

Reclaiming an Idea: Just like Anne was pleasantly surprised to rediscover and reclaim clothing she had forgotten about, our writers are often excited to revive an idea tucked away in their notebook. Mary sometimes provides students with five gold star stickers to ceremoniously place beside ideas they want to reclaim and develop, ideas that have gold-star potential to the writer. Time is then provided for students to take one of those starred ideas and light it up through writing. When students are stumped for an idea, encourage them to search for those stand-out stars in their notebook.

Revisiting a Strategy: In Chapter 3, we shared powerful writing strategies for mining our lives for writing ideas. Activities included using a memento to spark writing, writing about unforgettable people, exploring destinations known and unknown in writing. The power of these activities lies in doing them again but in a slightly different way.

Curiosity Drives the Writer

In 2018, the *Harvard Business Review* dedicated an entire issue to the topic of curiosity. In the article "The Business Case for Curiosity" Francesca Gino shares, "Most of the breakthrough discoveries and remarkable inventions throughout history, from flints for starting a fire to self-driving cars, have something in common: They are the result of curiosity. The impulse to seek new information and experiences and explore novel possibilities is a basic human attribute" (Gino, 2018).

Tapping into students' innate sense of curiosity about different topics, subjects, and issues honors their wonders and values their inquisitiveness. It is a source of powerful writing. Provide time for students to think, seek, investigate, research, and write about topics that intrigue them. It sends the message that their interests and thinking matter! So flood your classroom regularly with a variety of high-interest nonfiction texts and magazines collected by your school librarian. Encourage students to explore these texts whenever they have free time, and to be on the lookout for topics that spark their curiosity and have writing potential. We prominently post in our classroom an anchor chart listing suitable and engaging websites to ignite interest: *Wonderopolis, DOGO News, National Geographic Kids, BrainPOP, CBC Kids: How Stuff Works*, etc. Writers are encouraged to curate their curiosities into a list and track and record different topics, subjects, and issues they may want to write about in their notebooks.

Get Outside

The feel of the sun warming your body, gentle drops of rain flowing down your face; the sound of birds conversing in the trees, the buzz in the bushes of cicadas; the distinctive smell of dried leaves being burned, the aroma of the earth thawing in the spring. Our senses come to life when we are in nature. So take writers outside where their senses can be awoken and kindled by the beauty and splendor around them. Research reveals that

> …being in nature, or even viewing scenes of nature, reduces anger, fear, and stress and increases pleasant feelings. Exposure to nature not only makes you feel better

emotionally, it contributes to your physical well-being." (University of Minnesota, 2016)

Taking time to break out from the confines of your classroom opens up a world of writing possibilities for students. Here are some simple experiences that you can offer writers.

Cloud Watching: Take a moment to lie on the grass and examine the clouds. Look closely to discover hidden images that emerge from their ever-changing shapes. What we see is unique to our imagination and perception, and can become a stimulus for writing. A dinosaur, a dragon, a person's face: the possibilities are endless.

Sense Walk: Allow your five senses to be stimulated as you silently immerse yourself in your surroundings. Encourage students to note in writing the sights, sounds, and scents around them as they stroll the streets in their school community.

Moment in Nature: Every week on CBS Sunday Morning, a one-minute segment entitled Moment in Nature is featured. These short, unscripted videos immerse the viewer in nature—a conservation area or a national park—and feature animals in their natural habitat. So fire up the projector to enjoy the sights and sounds of our world and be compelled to write!

Bird Watching: The internet abounds with live cams featuring various species around the world in their natural habitat. In particular, we enjoy the variety of bird cams showcased on the Cornell Lab of Ornithology website (www.allaboutbirds.org). Students are captivated by the changing scenes and are amazed that they can watch events unfold in real time. Before you know it, students will be committing the scene to paper.

A Picture is Worth a Thousand Words: Google *National Geographic Nature Images* or go to Nat Geo's 46 Unbelievably Gorgeous Nature Photos To Get You Outside. You will be spellbound by the quantity and quality of awe-inspiring images at your fingertips. Select a variety of images, print in color, and distribute to students to investigate independently or with a peer. They will not be at a loss for words when viewing these images!

The Habit of Planning

Variety is the Spice of Life

> *Anne*
>
> Recently I binge-watched the History Channel mini-series *The Food That Built America*. The stories of renowned food tycoons, such as John and Will Kellogg, Henry Heinz, C. W. Post, and Milton Hershey are re-enacted in this informative program. In particular, the story of Milton Hershey captivated me, as I am a certifiable choco-holic. I find it impossible to envision a world where chocolate does not exist in its milk chocolate form, where there is no savoring and enjoying melt-in-your-mouth chocolate in its many manifestations. Cashews, peanuts, almond, brittle, coconut, caramel, mint, nugget, cookie wafers—you name it, paired with chocolate it tastes divine. Smartly and elegantly featuring a variety of delectable treats in glass showcases entices us to eagerly sample and enjoy.

That is what our writers need—to sample and try different choices of form, format, craft technique, etc. In writing conferences, take the opportunity to encourage particular students to venture outside their writing preferences and try something new. As well, consider spotlighting specific formats that are being overlooked as a class and for particular students.

What Are Your Writing Super Powers

Marvel and DC superheroes have unique attributes, talents, and qualities that set them apart, and so do our writers. Our role is to support them in discovering, acknowledging, and celebrating the writing superpowers that they have developed throughout the year. For example, some students are talented at writing a particular format, such as comics or poetry, while others are talented at injecting humor and suspense into texts. During writing conferences, support authors in uncovering their writing talents and gifts:

- Is there a particular form of writing that you have a flair for creating? (Narrative, Descriptive, Expository, Persuasive)
- What formats are you drawn to and enjoy writing in?
- Which stage of the writing process do you excel at? (generating ideas, drafting, revising, editing, publishing)
- Do you infuse your writing with certain craft techniques? Which one would you consider yourself to be a master of?
- Are you someone who listens with a discerning ear and can offer thoughtful feedback to fellow writers?
- Do you read with a critical eye and can spot a spelling mistake or grammatical error with ease?

Knowing your own talents and gifts as a writer and member of the classroom writing community supports everyone in being respected and appreciated for what they know, can do, and are able to offer fellow writers. You might consider publicly sharing the gifts of each writer in your class on a desktop placard that can be posted when students are writing. It sends a message to writers that we are all talented in diverse ways, and can learn from and support each other in this writing community.

Strategies for Fueling a Writing Life Outside of School

Thought Jot Books: Providing students with flip notepads is a powerful way to encourage them to always be on the lookout for writing ideas that can be quickly recorded for future reference. This inexpensive tool becomes an invaluable idea bank for future writing and is small enough to transport in a pocket.

Traveling Notebooks: In Mary's vibrant and flourishing writing community, she encourages and permits her students to write whenever and wherever the idea strikes. This includes allowing students to take their notebooks between home and school if they wish, with the commitment to bring it back to class each day. Depending on your class and school community, this might not be a viable option; in these cases, we encourage you to provide each student with a duotang filled with paper for writing. These can be brought back to class for sharing.

WWW (Wow Writing Wednesdays): We know that our developing writers are eager to share finished and unfinished pieces with their writing community for feedback, comments, and recognition. Encourage students to sign up on a posted list on Wednesday morning if they wish to share writing they have done at home. Whenever you have a few minutes, invite an author to the author's chair to share, showcasing their writing and celebrating their accomplishments.

The Habit of Acting: Thinking

Writing DNA Card

All developing writers have their own unique writing DNA. Adapting the DNA Inventory from Mrs. Mac's Kinders (2018), we use a DNA card to help our students reflect about themselves as writers; see page 137 for the Writing DNA Cards template. This flexible frame can be used and reused with different prompts to illicit a variety of valuable information.

Desires: What are your areas of interest? (topics, themes, forms, formats) What desires and dreams do you have as a writer? (*To make my readers laugh; To document and record special memories; To make more time for writing.*) Are there particular areas you'd like to explore in your writing life? (*memorable moments; writing in detail; writing from a different perspective.*)

Needs: What do you need from me to support you as a writer? (*To read my writing; To give me feedback; Match me with mentor text to develop craft.*) What tools do you access to assist you in your writing? (mentor texts, thesaurus, modeled writing, anchor charts, chrome books, dictionary) Identify a few areas that need your attention. (*planning my writing; spend more time writing outside school; jot down my ideas before I lose them; pay more attention to craft techniques.*)

Abilities: What abilities, talents, and gifts do you have that will support you as a writer? (*I have many seeds in my writer's notebook; I've got a knack for crafting poetry; I'm always willing to revisit and improve my writing.*) What do you want your reader to notice? (*That I'm great at the craft technique of show don't tell; That my published piece is very different from my first draft; That my piece is organized and makes sense; That I avoid overused words like "said," "walk," "happy," etc.*)

Quote Me

You cannot seem to go into any housewares or home goods store without seeing beautifully framed quotes for sale. A well-crafted statement seems to provide a bit of inspiration, give motivation to carry on, and have a lasting impact on our world. According to Ward Farnsworth, dean of the University of Texas School of Law and author of *Farnsworth's Classical English Rhetoric*, there is power in words. Farnsworth says that people have an "appetite for well-expressed wisdom, motivational or otherwise." Capitalize on the power of language to encourage, move, excite, persuade, and inspire by engulfing students in powerful quotes about writing from both influential and unknown personalities. The internet abounds with sites filled with quotes to choose from, but here a few of our favorite quotes.

- Sample quotes to share with young writers:

  "Start writing, no matter what. The water does not flow until the faucet is turned on." Louis L'Amour

  "Don't tell me the moon is shining; show me the glint of light on broken glass." Anton Chekhov

  "Everybody walks past a thousand story ideas every day. The good writers are the ones who see five or six of them. Most people don't see any." Orson Scott Card

- Tanny McGregor shares the following quotes about writing in her excellent book *Genre Connections*:

  "A poet is, before anything else, a person who is passionately in love with language." W.H. Auden

  "Fiction is life with the dull bits left out." Clive James

  "Facts are to the mind what food is to the body." Edmund Burke

- Quotes to share with younger writers from the book *Writing Radar: Using Your Journal to Snoop Out and Craft Great Stories* by Jack Gantos:

  "Take the expression 'I can read you like a book'. Well, you are a book on the inside. Writing just turns you inside out, and all your thoughts become words on the page."

  "Reading good books turns on the powerful Writing Radar story-finding talent within you."

  "When you get a good idea write it down or you will lose it. In other words, don't put money in a pocket with a hole in it."

  "'Nothing interesting ever happens to ME!' This is the all-ages writer's lament. Yet with a little prodding, some well-directed questions, and some prompts, most writers soon find that interesting things do happen to them—and either they were not paying attention or they just didn't fully trust that their personal experiences were worth writing about."

Additional quotes to share with young writers can be found on various websites, including The Writing Cooperative: https://writingcooperative.com/18-motivational-quotes-to-bring-out-the-writer-in-you-ea3e61c93734

Consider dividing your class into small groups and distributing one typed quote to each group for discussion. Ask students to mine the quote for meaning: What is it saying? What is the author trying to teach you/tell you? How do you relate as a writer to this statement? Once groups have had a chance to investigate their quote, have each group share their quote and thinking with the entire class. Alternatively, post each quote prominently on charts around the room; students can travel in small groups to think, talk, and graffiti their ideas on each chart. This brainstorming activity can be followed by a conversation that highlights the thinking, connections, and notes any *aha!*s that pop off the page. Some students will be eager to record their favorite quote in their writer's notebook to reflect on and cherish.

Photo Elicitation

In *photo elicitation*, visuals are used to elicit comments and responses from viewers. Images can include stimulating photographs, paintings, cartoons, etc. This interview method was developed in 1957 by photographer and researcher John Collier and has been used in many different ways. At its core, photo elicitation speaks to our affective domain, as our brains are more adept at processing visuals or visuals with text rather than text alone. Use this effective strategy to have students think about writing, their writing life, and their identity. Consider purchasing stock images or merely select images online that you think will speak to your students. Once visuals have been color printed, prompt your writers: *Select an image that represents you as a writer and your experiences with writing from the selected images*. Provide students an opportunity to think critically and reflectively about their chosen image and to write a response to the prompt. Offering students a chance to explore and reflect on themselves as a writer is imperative; it enables them to think about their growth, development, and progress as a writer in a tangible way.

The Habit of Acting: Sharing

Shout Outs

Writer Shout Outs invite classmates to endorse the writing of fellow students publicly in the form of recommendation cards. After publishing a major piece, have students exchange their work with a peer and complete a Shout Out card recommending the piece to others. Post the completed cards with the published work in the hall. You will be amazed at the buzz this display will generate among students who are eager to read the latest releases!

The Habit of Goal-Setting

In our classrooms, students have developed the ability to be highly reflective writers. They draft with a reader's ear, listening to how text sounds, hearing the way in which words flow, and considering if their message is conveyed eloquently. By positioning themselves frequently in the place of the audience, they write from a place of thoughtfulness and intention. Habitually doing this assists them in setting goals, achieving them, and drafting new ones. Taking time to celebrate the accomplishments and growth of our writers in frequent and public ways is essential. Validating the time, effort, and energy they have invested in growing as writers needs to be recognized. We're not talking stickers, certificates, or goodie bags, but instead an opportunity for them to monitor and reflect, and for our community to applaud their achievements. Sharing of successes sustains and nourishes our writers. Here are a few ways you can celebrate student writing commitment in manageable and effective ways.

Celebration Circle

Consider facilitating a free-writing celebration circle every couple of weeks. Have writers bring their Writer's Notebooks to the circle and orally share their work/life as writers. Encourage them to state their goal, share some writing, identify the concrete actions they took to meet that goal, and any lessons learned. This informal and spontaneous sharing provides momentum for writers to always be striving to become better writers by investing time and energy into free writing.

My Writing Journey

During writing conferences, we want students to reflect on their own development, growth, and learning. Initially we support students by sharing our observations and the key attributes we see in them as writers. As we develop a trusting relationship with our writers, they are more open and receptive to receiving and applying feedback to their work. We are able to comment critically, since students see us as fellow writers, as colleagues able to guide them to be more effective writers. Once students gain experience and comfort engaging in conversations about their work, they begin to actively contribute their own opinions, reflections, and insights to the conversation. Our guiding prompt is always *What have you learned about yourself as a writer lately?* Depending on the age of your students, record or have them record their key learning on an ongoing Writing Journey Card.

Challenge Yourself

Thanksgiving, Christmas, Family Day Weekend, March Break, Easter, Victoria Day long weekend—before each extended break during the school year, take time before the bell rings and students stream out the door to remind your writers that this gift of time will provide them with endless writing ideas and stimulation. They need to be on the look out for funny, touching, exciting, surprising, unexpected events, all memorable moments worth recording. Like the time Anne's Yellow Labrador Mac walked off with the entire mega-pack of marshmallows on Victoria day weekend. The bandit was discovered with a sugary mass smeared across his face and coat. Your instructions might sound like this:

> *It is my hope that, over the holidays, you will be on the lookout for seed ideas and that you will carve out time to immerse yourself in writing! I am asking that you set a personal writing challenge for yourself. It could be about the ideas you want to collect, or the formats you want to explore, or even the amount of time you want to commit to writing each day. It's all up to YOU! What matters most is that you stretch yourself as a writer and increase your competence, confidence, and writing motivation through practice.*

On the first day back after the holidays, have students share their personal challenge and captured moments with their writing community.

Writing Open House

Our partners in education are our students' parents. It is essential that we welcome them into our learning environment on an ongoing basis so that they can bear witness to the learning community we have established. Twice a year, students invite their parents to our community to share and articulate their growth as a student. Parents are given guiding questions to facilitate the conversation with their child. Here are a few of the questions we provide our students to highlight their life as a writer:

- What are the unique characteristics of our writing community?

> To ensure your students have a productive conference, have them practice answering these questions with a partner in advance.

- What are some of the traits of an effective writer?
- Describe yourself as a writer.
- How have you changed as a writer this past year? Explain a few ways you have grown.

Instruct students:

Take a select number of published pieces from your writing folder and Writer's Notebook. Share with your parent(s)/guardian(s) how you selected each text. Explain, "I have chosen to share with you this piece because..." After you have shared your writing, ask your parents to comment on your piece. Were they hooked by your lead? Did they notice your detailed descriptions? Were pictures created in their mind? What word phrases popped out at them?

> Pause and Ponder: How will you continue to develop the habits of your writers over the course of the year?

Be sure to have students speak about what they are proud of in each piece, perhaps calling their parents' attention to something they didn't notice (craft techniques, sentence fluency, the presentation format, etc.)

Make the *Why* of Writing Visible

Committed and avid writers can answer the question "Why write?" They are able to offer a variety of reasons why writing is important to them and for them. We have highlighted the following reasons to write: to express our thoughts and feelings; to record and document memories; for pleasure and enjoyment; to clarify our thinking and ideas; to share knowledge and experiences; to become better writers; to become more appreciative readers; to share valuable life lessons; to communicate with DEEP (Describe, Explain, Entertain, and Persuade). In Chapter 5, we shared activities to provide you and your students with ongoing experiences that illustrate reasons to write. These activities are not intended to be one-and-done, but rather need to be constantly referred to and invested in so that developing writers internalize the will to write. Here are three additional activities to make the *why* of writing visible.

Connecting Our Writing to *Why*

After students have finished writing a text, it's beneficial to have them think metacognitively about the writing process and their work. Reflecting on how they have advanced as a writer from crafting text, based on the writing reasons, keeps the *why* at the forefront. Understanding the range of reasons that writing is important, valuable, and beneficial to them cements their commitment to writing. Every once in a while, if students are sharing a finished piece during a writing conference, have them respond to the following prompt:

Identify with a check mark which writing reasons you benefitted from while writing this piece:
☐ I expressed my thoughts and feelings.
☐ I recorded and documented memories.
☐ I wrote for pleasure and enjoyment.
☐ I clarified my thinking and ideas.
☐ I shared my knowledge and experiences.

☐ I became a better writer.
☐ I became a more appreciative reader.
☐ I shared valuable life lessons.
☐ I communicated by DEEP (Describing, Explaining, Entertaining, and Persuading).

Validate your thinking by showing me where in your piece you have done these things.

Writing Rants

Tuesday nights, 8:00 pm, CBC—it's time for the Rick Mercer Report! For 15 seasons, this Newfoundland comedian and political satirist entertained Canadians weekly. Each show followed a similar format and always included a rant. These rapid-fire two-minute monologues about current issues were filmed while Mercer walked up and down graffiti-strewn Rush Lane in Toronto. Viewers sat back and enjoyed the fast-paced ride as the comedic wordsmith persuaded you to his way of thinking. Have students channel their personal powers of persuasion and provide them a similar opportunity to make the *why* of writing visible to others by creating their own rant videos. Provide partners with a tablet and have them select an app to record their voice and image (e.g., iMovie, Adobe Spark, Green Screen, Flipgrid). In the video, students will use the writing reasons to motivate and illustrate the importance of writing to other students. Go public by sharing these videos with other classes and parents. Once you have been bitten by the writing bug, you cannot be silenced. You want to inspire, motivate, and persuade others to write. Let your students do the same.

Author Reveal

While we sit drafting this final chapter, we are no longer able to write across from one another at the kitchen table. The recent global COVID-19 pandemic has astonishingly altered every single aspect of our lives, but especially our ability to interact with others. One positive that has emerged during forced confinement has been the abundance of authors for children and young adults reaching out to readers via YouTube to share their stories chapter by chapter. The accessibility of these writers to their audience and their willingness to read aloud their beloved stories to children has been remarkable.

For many students, the author is often a faceless entity whose name on the book cover is insignificant and irrelevant. But change that by ensuring that students know and celebrate the mentors who inspire and motivate them to read and write. The books that have touched our minds and moved our hearts are truly gifts. The authors of these gems deserve our thanks and praise. Early in the school year, we purposefully write a thank-you note to an author whose book we have read as a class, typically a read-aloud, that has been a mentor text to writers. We model how to acknowledge and thank an author for their story and share how it affected us personally. Sometimes, we have been lucky enough to receive a personal response in return. The excitement and thrill this gives growing readers/writers is priceless.

When students genuinely and enthusiastically share their love for a mentor text with you during a writing conference, encourage them to write their own thank-you notes to that author. Provide them with an assortment of thank-you cards to choose from and a special pen with which to write their sincere appreciation.

Pause and Ponder: How do you plan to make the *why* of writing visible to your students throughout the year?

Author websites and Twitter accounts provide easy access to author contact information. Mail these notes with a return address and hope for a response.

Provide What Students Need to Write

One of the things we look forward to every August is the anticipation we feel as back-to-school approaches. The commercials on TV feature parents skipping with glee up and down school-supply–filled aisles to the strains of "It's the Most Wonderful Time of the Year." If you're a teacher, you might feel this way too. Your pulse accelerates at the thought of a fresh pack of Mr. Sketch smelly markers. Sharpening all your new pencils to pointy perfection puts a smile on your face. Entering your freshly scrubbed classroom fills you with glee, and figuring out room layout is exhilarating. "New" and "fresh" are synonymous with "back to school." But why limit those feelings to the end of August and early September? Hold on to them and inject that energy throughout the year. Avoid tools and spaces appearing stale, tired, or dated. Our writers deserve things that are fresh, vibrant, and current. If you make a few subtle changes over the course of the year, your writing environments stay attractive, purposeful, and engaging. Subtle ways can make a strong impact.

Staying Current

Each year new authors and titles emerge and get a tremendous amount of publicity from the literary community. On Twitter we follow Mr. Schu Reads, Margin Notes, Harper Collins Children's Books, Children's Book Shelf, Celebrate Science, Canadian Children's Book Centre, and The Horn Book, to name a few that keep us abreast of the hottest new titles. Their feeds light up with cover reveals, trailers, and reviews. Shiny, new titles hold an appeal to readers as they provoke a sense of excitement and anticipation. We want to be one of the first people to get our hands on that book! To create added anticipation and buzz around an upcoming title's release, post a picture of the cover with its release date. Let the countdown begin!

Exposing students to quality literature is our responsibility and our extreme pleasure as educators. Over the last number of years, new topics and themes in text have emerged, themes that were relatively unheard of a decade ago. Included are systemic injustice, race and diversity, immigrant and refugee stories, Indigenous experiences, mental wellness, physical disabilities, poverty, and gender identity. To validate and honor our diverse and ever-changing population, we must commit to ensuring that all students see themselves represented and reflected in text. Intentionally ensuring that collections are current and contain materials that mirror our class, community, and world builds understanding and empathy. As well, injecting classrooms with literature that tugs at the heart strings, intrigues the mind, and propels students to write their own stories is imperative. These texts also serve as vital mentors to our developing writers for ideas and craft. As our students grow and change as readers and writers, so must the books in our classroom libraries.

Writer Bio

Another strategy to support the development of your writing community is celebrating the writers in your class by spotlighting them. Feature a writer in the class for a week. Photograph the selected student on a Friday and ask them about

> Their Habits: Where do you get your ideas from? What topics do you enjoy writing about? What are your preferred formats to write? What are your favorite writing spots in the classroom and at home? Who do you enjoy sharing your writing with?
>
> Their Tools: Do you have preferences for what you like to write with? Pen/pencil, paper or computer?
>
> Free/Structured: What do you enjoy about free writing? How does structured writing help you develop as a writer?

As well, ask the student to select two or three pieces of text they would like to showcase, something interesting, engaging, thought-provoking, a must-read.

On the following Monday, start with a flattering introduction of the featured writer. Share all the wonderful things you have uncovered about them; consider referring to their writer survey, their I Am a Writer Who… poem, and notes from writing conferences. After pumping up the author in front of the class, ask them to reveal each of their writing selections and share details of their writing life. Prominently display these pieces with the student's photograph. If time permits, have the student share their selections as read-alouds throughout the week.

Conference Call

The power of a writing conference is that it enables you to precisely tailor your instruction and feedback to the specific writer you are working with, rather than providing general, broad feedback to the entire class.

As teachers, we often take notes of what we shared, discussed and explored so we can refer to them at subsequent conferences and when assessing student work. An I Can… Personal Revision/Editing List can support young writers in having the same sort of documentation with them when drafting, crafting, and revising text; see page 138 for I Can… template. At the end of a writing conference, allow a minute for the student to jot down on their I Can… list the writing tips and tricks they will apply and be responsible for in their writing going forward. This scaffolded level of support is key in writers remembering, applying, and owning the feedback given. Students keep this personalized list in their writing folder for easy access and it should accompany them to each writing conference.

Another idea is to have students complete a reflection form when submitting major writing pieces for assessment. Sentence stems, such as *What I learned about myself as a writer; I am proud of…; What I really want you to notice in this piece is…*, are great ways to get students to recognize that their writing ability can change from piece to piece, that their process ebbs and flows depending on the topic/purpose/audience/format, and that reflection is an essential part of cultivating a writing life.

Publishing Centre

Celebrating young writers by publishing their work provides them with authentic real-life purpose for writing.

> *Mary*
>
> I fondly remember the Springfield Press, a school-wide publishing company serving students in one of my former schools. This business ran like a fine-tuned machine and had many valuable employees: moms, dads, and grandparents worked tirelessly to type, assemble, bind, and deliver published work back to students. With guidance from their teacher, students could select pieces of their writing and complete the Springfield Press Publishing Instructions form, outlining format and layout. Revised, edited writing and completed instructions were then sealed in a brown manila envelope and placed in the Springfield Press's drop-off bin. After a short period of waiting, each student's typed and bound work was returned according to their author specifications. The excitement, joy, and pride students felt was palpable when they held their published writing in their hands.

Pause and Ponder: How will you update your tools and space to ensure that they are fresh, vibrant, and current throughout the year?

Times have changed since those early days of the Springfield Press, but we believe publishing student writing allows young writers to personally and fully experience the authorship cycle. Unfortunately, for many teachers and students, the task of publishing writing is daunting, tedious, and time-consuming. But the rewards to our students' writing lives are great, so put out a Help Wanted notice. Seek out school volunteers who are always ready and willing to help, look for keyboarders who wish to work from home at times convenient to them, and start your own school's publishing company. It won't be long before the drop-off bin will be erupting with the work of your young writers!

Maintaining Momentum

With the goal of nourishing and sustaining our writers throughout the year, in this chapter we have revisited each essential step for cultivating passionate writers. We hope that the tips and ideas shared for sustaining and maintaining the momentum of your writers inspire you to create your own customized and tailored activities. Cultivating the will to write in developing writers is something we must invest in on an ongoing basis in intentional ways. Naturally, it will take time. Surely, it will take effort. Absolutely, it will take energy. But just like trees, our writers will not grow, blossom, or mature without a caring and diligent horticulturist—and that's you!

The Writer I Was/The Writer I Am

Name: _____

I used to _____

Now I _____

I used to _____

Now I _____

I used to _____

Now I _____

I used to _____

Now I _____

I used to _____

Now I _____

I am _____ and I am a changed writer!

WRITING IS POWERFUL

Writing DNA Cards

My Writing DNA   Name: _____

Desires   _____
               _____
               _____

Needs   _____
               _____
               _____

Abilities   _____
               _____
               _____

My Writing DNA   Name: _____

Desires   _____
               _____
               _____

Needs   _____
               _____
               _____

Abilities   _____
               _____
               _____

I Can…

My Personal Revision/Editing Checklist

Name: _____

I can…

- _____
 _____

- _____
 _____

- _____
 _____

- _____
 _____

- _____
 _____

- _____
 _____

- _____
 _____

- _____
 _____

Final Thoughts

In *Cultivating Writers* we have offered you our best thinking and work to nurture passionate writers. We hope that our research-informed and unique response will support you in reflecting and refining your thinking about writing instruction, and that you are now filled to the brim with your own ideas for fostering the will to write in your students. Take these ideas, mull them over, tweak them, try them out—and be prepared to be astounded by the transformative power of addressing the will to write in students. Your young writers will be compelled to pick up the pen because they know they have something to say, know their voice matters, and know the power of the written word to change the world.

We once heard a speaker say at a conference that, as a teacher, she had a lot of *If-only...* years:

> You know what we mean. *If only* someone had told me. *If only* I had tried that. *If only* I had done that. *If only* I had known that before.

We remember watching countless educators around the room nod their heads in shared agreement. And we, too, have had a lot of *If-only...* years. What conscientious teacher hasn't?

We wish that when we started teaching we knew what we know now:
- that just as important as teaching writing skills is fostering the will
- that I, as the teacher, have a crucial role in creating a community of writers
- that, as the lead writer, I can inspire and motivate students to develop the will to write
- that fostering wilful writing requires intentional instruction as outlined in the six essential steps we introduced to you to in this book.

Our hope is that after reading *Cultivating Writers* you have fewer *If-only...* years, that you are confident addressing the will to write in your classroom, and that you are supported by the activities outlined in each chapter to create a vibrant community of writers. You can indeed teach the will to write if you ground the development of your writing community in the six essential steps.

As we write these last lines we are in the midst of a global pandemic. Our world has been turned upside-down and life as we know it is in turmoil and incredibly uncertain. Stress, worry, and anxiety seem to be our constant companions as news feeds overwhelm us with updates and reports. However, Twitter, Facebook, Instagram, and other social media are bursting with feel-good stories, strategies for coping, and ways to connect virtually with family and friends. A bright light in the darkness has been the words of hope, inspiration, and encouragement that authors, both acclaimed and unknown, have posted on websites, shared on blogs, and forwarded to countless others. Emails from loved ones checking in, sharing a joke or updates on their new stay-at-home lifestyle, are comforting. Cards and letters with kind messages let us know we have not been forgotten. Each of these written communications has purpose and value—and are lifelines during this difficult time. Someone, somewhere, took the time, invested the energy, and put forth the creativity to craft every story, poem, message, joke, anecdote, report, article.

How many people are seeking solace and comfort in the pages of a book? How many people are choosing to escape their current reality from the comfort of their easy chair? How many people are buoyed up by comforting and encouraging messages from others? At the same time, how many of us have been compelled to pick up a pen and document our own stories during this unprecedented time? How many of us have reached out in writing to a relative, friend, or loved one? How many of us have calmed our minds and settled our emotions by taking time to journal? We are thankful for the ability to write ourselves and are grateful for the written word of others. It must be repeated again and again: cultivating a writing life matters.

Acknowledgments

"Gratitude teaches us to appreciate the rainbow and the storm."—Christina G. Hibbert, Psy.D.

As we write these final words, we wonder who will actually read them. For many, this page is a secondary add-on, but to us it is a sacred space to express our gratitude for the both the rainbows and the storms we have experienced over the last year writing this book. Just as it takes a combination of colors to create the beautiful splendor of the rainbow, many people have contributed and supported us in different ways throughout this endeavor. We would be remiss if we did not acknowledge the expertise and work of others who inspired, informed, and elevated our understanding as writing teachers and writers: Calkins, Dorfman & Cappelli, Fletcher, Graves, Hale, Kittle, Lamott, Murray, Tompkins, Rog, Routman, etc. The voices of these authors are scattered across the pages of this book like the rainbow across the sky.

A heartfelt thank-you goes out to Cara Rae Clements, Stephanie Cook, Sabrina Marr, and Jenny Moreland-Fife, who field-tested lessons in their classrooms and offered us valuable feedback that influenced our thinking. In particular, we are grateful for the work undertaken by Jenny and Sabrina with their writers that are featured in this book. We appreciate the open-door policy that Cara afforded Mary as a writer-in-residence in her Grade 3 class. The ability to teach, model, conference, talk, and write alongside students freely was a true pleasure and gift. And let's not forget our dear friend and fellow book addict Jane Baird, who was always a text or phone call away with a thoughtful book recommendation. Every literacy teacher needs a Jane!

All our conversations at the outset of writing this book centred around student voice. Children must uncover and discover that their voice is important, is significant, and has value. What they think, dream, wonder, hope, know, experience, notice, and feel matters, and is worth writing about. We are grateful for the countless students we have written for, with, and alongside. Without knowing it, you have made us better teachers and writers. It is our constant hope that every child in our classroom communities knows the power of their words and the influence they hold in their pen.

In the spirit of transparency, there were times when the sky went dark, storm clouds loomed, and the rains fell. The hugeness of the task, the commitment and conviction it takes to stick with it, and periods of writer's block all took a toll on us as writers and also on those we love and long to be with. The time, effort, and energy we put into this passion project has taken us away from our families and friends, who endured our absence from many social events, listened patiently as we worked out our thinking, and offered endless encouragement and reassurance. Like them, we are ecstatic that *Cultivated Writers* is now completed. After the storms, the rainbow is now decorating our sky.

Finally, we must thank Mary Macchiusi for her steadfast support, encouragement, and interest in our thoughts and work. Through Pembroke, she once again has provided us an authentic audience for our ideas and writing. And to Kat Mototsune, our editor—your critical eye, writing expertise, and knowledge of effective presentation enhanced and enriched this book.

Professional Resources

Atwell, Nancie (1998) *In the Middle: New Understanding about Writing, Reading, and Learning, Second Edition.* Toronto, ON: Irwin.

Buckner, Aimee (2005) *Notebook Know-How: Strategies for the Writer's Notebook.* Portland, Maine: Stenhouse Publishers.

Calkins, Lucy and Harwayne, Shelley (1990) *Living Between the Lines.* Portsmouth, NH: Heinemann.

The Canadian Council on Learning (2016) *The Kindergarten Program.* Ontario Ministry of Education.

Chapman, Carolyn and King, Rita (2003) *Differentiated Instructional Strategies for Writing in the Content Areas.* Thousand Oaks, CA: Corwin Press Inc.

Culham, Ruth (2005) *6 + 1 Traits of Writing: Everything You Need to Teach and Assess Writing with this Powerful Model.* New York, NY: Scholastic Teaching Resources.

Digh, Patti (2014) *Your Daily Rock: A Daybook of Touchstones for Busy Lives.* Lanham, MD: Taylor Trade Publishing.

Dorfman, Lynne R. & Cappelli, Rose (2007) *Mentor Texts: Teaching Writing Through Children's Literature, K–6.* Portland, ME: Stenhouse Publishers.

Fletcher, Ralph (2017) *Joy Write.* Portsmouth, NH: Heinemann.

Fletcher, Ralph (1996) *Breathing In, Breathing Out: Keeping a Writer's Notebook*, Portsmouth, NH: Heinemann.

Fletcher, Ralph and Portalupi, JoAnn (2004) *Teaching the Qualities of Writing.* Portsmouth, NH: Heinemann.

Fletcher, Ralph (2003) *A Writer's Notebook: Unlocking the Writer Within You.* New York, NY: Harper Collins.

Farnsworth, Ward in Moran, Gwen (September 2015) *The Science Behind Why Inspirational Quotes Motivate Us* https://www.fastcompany.com/3051432/why-inspirational-quotes-motivate-us

Friedrich, Elizabeth (1996) *Leah's Pony.* Honesdale, PA: Boyds Mills Press.

Gallagher, Kelly (2008) *Improving Adolescent Writers* DVD-ROM. Portland, ME: Stenhouse Publishers.

Gallagher, Kelly (2003) *Reading Reasons: Motivational Mini-Lessons for Middle and High School,* Portland, ME: Stenhouse Publishers.

Gallozzi, Chuck (2009) "Benefits of Laughter" Published Saturday, April 18, Personal-Development.com

Gantos, Jack (2017) *Writing Radar: Using Your Journal To Snoop Out and Craft Great Stories.* New York, NY: Farrar, Straus and Giroux.

Gibson, Allison (Dec. 2017) "Where Do Writers Write" *The Huffington Post*, https://www.huffpost.com/entry/where-do-writers-write_b_592619

Gino, Francesca (September 2018) *The Business Case for Curiosity. Harvard Business Review* https://hbr.org/2018/09/curiosity

Graves, Donald (1983) *Writing: Teachers and Children at Work.* Portsmouth, NH: Heinemann.

Graves, Donald (1994) *A Fresh Look at Writing.* Portsmouth, NH: Heinemann.

Harvey, Stephanie & Goudvis, Anne (2007) *Strategies That Work: Teaching Comprehension for Understanding and Engagement*, Second Edition. Portland, ME: Stenhouse Publishers.

Heard, Georgia (2016) *Heart Maps: Helping Students Create and Craft Authentic Writing,* Portsmouth, NH: Heinemann.

Jamison Rog, Lori and Kropp, Paul (2004) *The Write Genre.* Markham, ON: Pembroke Publishers.

Kittle, Penny (2008) *Write Beside Them: Risk, Voice, and Clarity in High School Writing.* Portsmouth, NH: Heinemann.

Koch, Kenneth and Padgett, Ron (2000) *Wishes, Lies, and Dreams: Teaching Children to Write Poetry.* New York, NY: Harper Perennial.

Krashen, Stephen D. (2004) *The Power of Reading: Insights from the Research*, Second Edition. Portsmouth, NH: Heinemann.

Lamott, Anne (1995) *Bird by Bird: Some Instructions on Writing and Life.* New York, NY: Anchor.

Layne, Steven L. (2009) *Igniting a Passion for Reading: Successful Strategies for Building Lifetime Readers.* Portland, ME: Stenhouse Publishers.

Lundy, Kathleen Gould (2007) *Leap Into Literacy.* Markham, ON: Pembroke Publishers.

MacArthur, C.A., Graham, S., and Fitzgerald, J. (Editors) (2006) *Handbook of Writing Research* First Edition. New York, NY: Guilford.

Mallan, Kerry (1991) *Children as Storytellers.* Portsmouth, NH: Heinemann.

McGregor, Tanny (2013) *Genre Connections.* Portsmouth, NH: Heinemann.

Miller, Debbie (2008) *Teaching with Intention: Defining Beliefs, Aligning Practice, Taking Action.* Portland, ME: Stenhouse Publishers.

Mrs. Mac's Kinders (2018) *D.N.A. (Dreams, Needs, and Abilities) Inventories and their Power in the Classroom.* https://mrsmacskindergarten.blogspot.com/2018/04/dna-dreams-needs-and-abilities.html?m=1

Rief, Linda (2018) *The Quickwrite Handbook: 100 Mentor Texts to Jumpstart Your Students' Thinking and Writing.* Portsmouth, NH: Heinemann.

Rief, Linda (2007) *Inside the Writers-Readers Notebook.* Portsmouth, NH: Heinemann.

Rief, Linda (2003) *100 Quickwrites: Fast and Effective Freewriting Exercises That Build Students' Confidence, Develop Their Fluency, and Bring Out the Writer in Every Student: Grades 5 and Up.* New York, NY: Scholastic Teaching Resources.

Rog, Lori Jamison (2011) *Marvelous Minilessons for Teaching Intermediate Writing, Grades 4–6.* Newark, DE: International Reading Association.

Routman, Regie (2012) *Literacy and Learning Lessons from a Longtime Teacher.* Newark, DE: International Reading Association.

Schu, John (August 22, 2019) "Review of Kent State by Deborah Wiles" *Watch. Connect. Read.* http://mrschureads.blogspot.com/2019/08/kent-state-by-deborah-wiles.html

Seal, Moorea (2015) *The 52 Lists Project: A Year of Weekly Journaling Inspiration.* Seattle, WA: Sasquatch Books.

Smith, M.C. (nd) *The Benefits of Writing.* Center for the Interdisciplinary Study of Language and Literacy, Northern Illinois University. https://www.niu.edu/language-literacy/_pdf/the-benefits-of-writing.pdf

Stagg Peterson, Shelley and Swartz, Larry (2008) *Good Books Matter.* Markham, ON: Pembroke Publishers.

University of Minnesota "How Does Nature Impact Our Wellbeing?" Taking Charge of Your Health & Wellbeing. www.takingcharge.csh.umn.edu/how-does-nature-impact-our-wellbeing

Watts, Irene (1992) *Making Stories.* Markham, ON: Pembroke Publishers.

Whitaker, Charles (2006) "Best Practices in Teaching Writing" *Write in the Middle: A workshop for Middle School Teachers.* Retrieved on Feb 2015 from: http://www.learner.org/

Willis J. (2017) *Why All Students Should Write: A Neurological Explanation for Literacy* https://www.teachthought.com/literacy/why-all-students-should-write-a-neurological-explanation-for-literacy/

Wood Ray, Katie (1991) *Wondrous Words.* Urbana, IL: National Council of Teachers of English.

The Writing Centre (2020) "Reading Aloud" The University of North Carolina Chapel Hill. https://writingcenter.unc.edu/tips-and-tools/reading-aloud/

Index

alliteration, 72
anecdotes, 19
appreciative readers, 100–101
asking students, 102
authentic reading, 100–101
author reveal, 132–133
Author's Board
    described, 23–24
    students, 24
Author's Chair, 76
Author's Circle, 118
Authority List, 38

better writing
    described, 98–99
    free writing, 100
    prompt-based writing, 99–100
    quickwrites, 99
Block Writing
    described, 58–60
    sample brainstorms, 60
brand names, 72
Burning Questions / Cool Ideas, 55

celebration circle, 129–130
challenging yourself, 130
clarifying thinking
    described, 94–95
    listing learning, 96–97
    resident experts, 95–96
    Triple-C Card, 95
    using your voice, 97–98

    writing-in-the-real-world interview, 96
classroom arrangement
    full group, 104–106
    individual nook, 106
    priorities, 104
    proximity to other students, 105–106
    proximity to teacher, 105
    proximity to text, 105
    small groups, 106
classroom library
    appraising, 111–113
    described, 108–111
    mentor texts, 109–111
    must-have authors / texts, 109–110
    nonfiction, 112–113
    questions to ask, 111
    suggestions for building, 111–112
communication, 102
conferences, 113–114, 134
Craft Conversations, 77–78
curiosity, 124

describe, explain, entertain, and persuade (DEEP), 102
descriptive writing, 57
Destination Known / Unknown
    described, 40
    template, 51
Dig Up Buried Stories, 38

expectations, 11
expository writing, 57

expressing thoughts and feelings
    benefits, 88–89
    bursting onto the page, 89
    described, 88–89
    inside-out writing, 89–91

finding habit
    Burning Questions / Cool Ideas, 55
    curiosity, 124
    described, 54, 123–124
    getting outside, 124–125
    notebooks, 54–55
    reading, 56
    reclaiming an idea, 124
    rereading notebooks, 123–124
    revisiting a strategy, 124
flavorful formats, 71–72
formal sharing
    Author's Chair, 76
    Hot Off the Press, 76
    Lines that Linger, 77
Format Flea Market
    described, 56–57
    template, 82
format tracker, 57–58
free writing, 100, 102

getting outside
    bird watching, 125
    cloud watching, 125
    described, 124–125
    moment in nature, 125
    pictures, 125
    sense walk, 125
gift of writing
    giving, 87–88
    students, 121
Give One, Get One Lists
    described, 26
    template, 28
goal-setting
    celebration circle, 129–130
    challenge yourself, 130
    conversation starters, 113–114
    described, 78, 129
    My Writing Journey, 130
    Passionate / Proficient Writer Anchor Chart, 79
    setting writing goals, 80–81
    writing open house, 130–131
Goodbyes Are Never Easy, 122
guest of honor, 18

habits for writers
    described, 123
    finding, 123–125
    goal-setting, 129–131
    planning, 125–127
    sharing, 129
    thinking, 127–129
Hand Map, 38
heart books, 70
Heart Map, 38
Hot Off the Press, 76
humor, 70–71, 92–94

I Am a Writer Who…
    described, 32–33
    template, 50
I Am From, 42–43
I Can… Personal Revision / Editing List
    described, 134
    template, 138
If You're Not From…, 44
informal sharing
    Craft Conversations, 77–78
    Put Down the Pen, 77
    Trading Texts, 77
inside-out writing, 89–91
instruction, 12
interest inventory
    described, 31–32
    template, 45–46

lack of writing will
    expectations and, 11
    high goals and, 12–13
    instruction and, 11
    statistics, 10–11
    structure and, 12
    underlying causes, 11–13
    writing skill and, 8, 10
laughter, 70–71, 92–94
Let's Make a Deal
    carving out time, 62–63
    catching and capturing, 63
    described, 61–62
    time commitment, 62
life lessons, 101–102
Lines that Linger, 77
list making, 18
listing learning, 96–97
Love It / Loathe It, 38

magic of three, 72
mementos, 41–42
memories, 91–92
mentor texts, 68
mentors / mentoring, 25–26
momentum, 135
music, 91–92
My Writing Journey, 130
My Writing Publication Record, 116

narrative writing, 57
new releases / writing
    described, 120
    featuring, 120
    gift of writing, 121
    release party, 120
notebooks
    rereading, 123–124
    tapping into, 54–55
    traveling, 126
    writers', 34–37

operation notebook investigation, 44
oral storytelling
    build a story, 73–74
    described, 73
    more than one story, 74
    picture prompt story, 73

Passionate / Proficient Writer Anchor Chart
    described, 79
    sample chart, 79
    setting writing goal, 80–81
Pencil Path
    described, 20–21
    students, 22
    template, 27
permission, 114–115
persuasive writing, 57
photo elicitation, 129
picture books, 69
plagiarism, 115
planning
    talents and gifts, 126
    variety, 125–126
    writing life outside school, 126–127
planning what to write
    Block Party, 58–60
    described, 56
    Format Flea Market, 56–57
    format tracker, 57–58

planning when to write
    carving out time to write, 62–63
    catching and capturing, 63
    described, 60–61
    Let's Make a Deal, 61–63
    time commitment, 62
planning where to write
    described, 63–64
    discussing, 64
play
    evolution of, 7
    problems with, 6
    unstructured, 6–7
pleasure and enjoyment
    books, 93
    described, 92–93
    enjoyment factor, 93–94
Precious Pages
    described, 22–23
    students, 23
presentation, 115
private places, 119
prompt-based writing, 99–100
proper nouns, 72
publication, 114
publishing centre, 135
Put Down the Pen, 77

quickwrites, 99
quotes, 127–128

reaction reading, 118–119
read-alouds
    described, 68–69
    flavorful formats, 71–72
    heart books, 70
    laughter / humor, 70–71
    picture books, 69
    stimulating writing, 71
    writers' adventures, 69–70
    writing, 119–120
reading
    authentic, 100–101
    habit, 68–72
    reaction reading, 118–119
    read-alouds, 68–72
    replicating favorite writers, 72
    sparking writing, 56
reading writing aloud, 119–120
reasons for writing
    author reveal, 132–133

connecting writing to, 131–132
described, 86–88, 131
writing rants, 132
reclaiming ideas, 124
recording and documenting memories
described, 91
music and, 91–92
write that down, 92
reflection form, 134
relationships, 123
release party, 120
repetition, 72
replicating favorite writers, 72
rereading notebooks, 123–124
resident experts, 95–96
revisiting strategies, 124

seasonal prompts, 122
sharing
described, 74–76
formal sharing, 76–77
informal sharing, 77–78
power of, 75
private versus public writing, 75–76
promoting writer, 75
reasons for, 74
shout outs, 129
sharing knowledge and experiences
described, 94–95
listing learning, 96–97
resident experts, 95–96
Triple-C Card, 95
using your voice, 97–98
writing-in-the-real-world interview, 96
sharing life lessons, 101–102
shout outs, 129
simile, 72
special events, 122
staying current, 133
stimulating writing, 71
structure, 12
supporting students
conferences, 134
publishing centre, 135
staying current, 133
writer bio, 134

talking
described, 73
oral storytelling, 73–74

tapping into students' lives
described, 121
supplementary seed ideas, 122–123
The Writer I Was / The Writer I Am, 122
writing status, 121–122
technology, 120
thinking
described, 64–65
photo elicitation, 129
quotes, 127–128
writing brain, 67
writing DNA card, 127
Writing Is…, 65
writing out loud, 65–67
thought jot books, 126
Times They Are a-Changing, 122
tools and supplies
described, 106–107
paper products, 107–108
storage, 108
writing utensils, 107
Trading Texts, 77
traveling notebooks, 126
Triple-C Card, 95

unforgettable people and pets, 39–40
using your voice, 97–98

vivid verbs, 72

When I Was Young, 43
whisper phones, 119
wilful writing habits
commitment, 53
described, 52–53
work in progress
Author's Circle, 118
described, 118
Reaction Reading, 118–119
Stuck in the Mud, 119
Wow Writing Wednesdays (WWW), 127
writer bio, 134
The Writer I Was / The Writer I Am
described, 122
template, 136
writer's notebook
cover creation, 36–37
described, 34
notebook tour, 34–36
sample letter, 49

writers
    replicating, 72
    self-driven, 7–8, 52
    skilled, 7
writing adventures, 69–70
Writing Bingo, 38
writing brain
    described, 67
    template, 83–84
writing community, 29–30
writing conferences, 113–114, 134
writing DNA (desires, needs, abilities) card
    described, 127
    template, 137
writing goals
    bookmark, 85
    described, 80–81
writing ideas
    Destination Known / Unknown, 40
    I Am From, 42–43
    If You're Not From…, 44
    mementos, 41–42
    mini-lessons, 38
    mining lives for, 37
    stimulating, 71
    operation notebook investigation, 44
    unforgettable people and pets, 39–40
    When I Was Young, 43
    writers in the house, 41
writing improvement
    described, 98–99
    free writing, 100
    prompt-based writing, 99–100
    quickwrites, 99
writing-in-the-real-world interview, 96
Writing Is…, 65
writing journey, 130
writing life
    anecdotes, 19
    Author's Board, 23–24
    developing, 117–121
    engaging in writing, 16
    expressing yourself, 19
    fostering, 15–20
    fueling outside school, 126–127
    guests of honor, 18–19
    list making, 18
    natural wonders, 20
    Pencil Path, 20–22
    Precious Pages, 22–23
    requirements, 16
    sharing in class, 20–24
    time and, 17
    writing mentor, 25–26
    writing territories, 17
writing mentor
    show and tell, 26
    teacher is writing, 25
writing open house, 130–131
writing out loud, 65–67
writing rants, 132
writing reasons
    author reveal, 132–133
    connecting writing to, 131–132
    described, 86–88, 131
    writing rants, 132
writing records
    acknowledgement and celebration, 114
    conferences, 113–114
    described, 113
    goal-setting, 113–114
    permission, 114–115
    plagiarism, 115
    presentation, 115
    publication, 114
    template, 116
    writing territories, 113
writing stamina, 98–99
writing status, 121–122
writing survey
    described, 32
    template, 47–48
writing territories
    described, 17
    tracing, 113
writing triage
    areas of knowledge, 31
    described, 30–31
    I Am a Writer Who…, 32–34
    interest inventory, 31–32
    writing survey, 32
writing will
    lack of, 8, 10–13
    nourishing, 117–135
    questions, 13–14
    requirements, 14
    steps to developing, 14

yoga, 15